LIVE YOUR BUCKET LIST

LIVE YOUR BUCKET LIST

SIMPLE STEPS TO IGNITE YOUR DREAMS, FACE YOUR FEARS AND LEAD AN EXTRAORDINARY LIFE, STARTING TODAY

Julia Goodfellow-Smith

Live Your Bucket List
Published by Julia Goodfellow-Smith

First published in 2021
Copyright © Julia Goodfellow-Smith

ISBN – hardcover: 978-0-85956-073-3
ISBN – paperback: 978-0-85956-074-0
ISBN – e-book: 978-0-85956-075-7
ISBN – audiobook: 978-0-85956-076-4

Live Your Bucket List is dedicated to my husband Mike, who has encouraged and supported me to live mine, and whose mantra I have successfully adopted:

'Julia, you've got this!'

Table of Contents

Introduction

'Life is to be lived as a magnificent adventure, or not at all.'

— Helen Keller, author and disability rights campaigner

Everything was damp – the air, my face, my clothes, my backpack. I had been walking in thick cloud and mizzle for miles, hood up and head down, trying to stay dry. I was suffering from severe anaemia, although I did not know it at the time. I thought that it was simple exhaustion that made my feet so heavy, my heart beat so fast and my lungs gasp for more oxygen. The mist veiled the view and muffled all sound. I had not seen or heard the sea for hours, even though I was walking the coast path. By rights, I should have felt dejected, bowed down by circumstance, yet I did not.

Because, after 25 years of dreaming, 6 months of planning and 52 days of walking, this was the day that I would fulfil my long-held dream to complete England's 630-mile South West Coast Path.

The end of the path was within reach, so however exhausted I was and whatever the weather was throwing at me, this was a magnificent day. After decades of procrastination, I had finally decided to walk the path, and I would finish it no matter what.

I had turned something that had been on my bucket list for decades into reality. Walking the South West Coast Path was no longer something I had always wanted to do. It was something that I had done. I used skills and techniques that I have built up throughout my life to smash through some of my limiting beliefs, learn new skills, become more self-reliant and extend my comfort zone.

In short, I expanded my horizons, and it was liberating.

Most people of a certain age have an 'I have always wanted to...' list. If you are younger, you might have a 'One day, I would love to...' list. This is your 'bucket list' – a list of things you want to do before a certain point in your life, or simply before you kick the bucket. Whether you want to learn another language, play in a rock band, run a marathon, write a book, or watch the sun set over Golden Gate Bridge, you will lead a much richer life if you start ticking things off your bucket list now. As you do, you will probably add new opportunities to your list, so there is no need to worry – you will never run out of dreams to fulfil.

It is a joy to dream. What could be more fun than sitting around a campfire with friends, talking about things you would love to do? Or putting the world to rights over a glass of wine?

Imagine how much greater it would feel, though, to actually achieve those dreams. Your campfire conversations would be full of anecdotes about a life well-lived.

This book gives you a step-by-step guide to living your bucket list. I have developed and refined this process over a lifetime, and I am delighted to be able to share it with you now.

Imagine setting off on a path that is heading towards your first bucket list dream. The path does not always head in a straight line. It has waymarkers that show you which way to go. Each step towards the waymarker is laid out clearly so that you know how to get there. The chapters in this book are your waymarkers pointing you in the right direction.

While you're walking along your path following the waymarkers, every now and again, you will reach a milestone. These mark significant moments in your journey. There are milestones within this book — igniting your dream, completing your plan, achieving your dream and reflecting on that achievement. These will help you know how far you've progressed along the way. They are moments for reflection and celebration as you get closer and closer to your goal of fulfilling your bucket list dream.

The first milestone is igniting your dream. If your bucket list is anything like mine, it will be overflowing with great ideas. The waymarkers on this leg of the journey will help you choose which dream you want to pursue, understand your reasons for wanting to do it, decide to act, and strengthen your resolve.

The second milestone is when you've completed your plan. It was not easy to achieve my bucket list dream of walking the South West Coast Path, but with good planning, it became manageable. Breaking down your dream into individual steps will make the whole process feel less daunting. Learning from others and planning for the worst will make things run more smoothly. And learning how to identify and use your superpowers while sidestepping your Achilles heels will increase your enjoyment. There are also waymarkers covering two of the biggest reasons that people do not turn their bucket list dreams into reality – time and money.

These first two milestones are like walking up the foothills towards the mountain of your dream. They represent the work you need to do in preparation for the final, glorious push to the summit.

Heading towards the third milestone of achieving your dream, the next set of waymarkers give you some life-hacks to apply while you are implementing your plan. These will help to make everything run more smoothly.

The fourth and final milestone covers something essential yet easily overlooked — reflection. It is important to congratulate yourself as you reach each waymarker, and check that you are still heading in the right direction. Reflection is also important at the end of your journey. It will help you to consolidate your memories and those things you have learnt along the way. That is where long-term satisfaction lies.

Each of the book's waymarkers starts with relevant stories from my journey, highlighted with learning points for you to consider. After that, there are individual steps for you to take to help you on your journey.

Download free templates to use for relevant steps from: www.juliags.com/liveyourbucketlist

Life is short, and time can slip by almost unnoticed. Bucket lists have a habit of growing, but having a long list of things you would like to do can be overwhelming. It can be fun to dream about the things on your bucket list, but actually turning them into reality is far more satisfying. Taking action on your bucket list allows to you live a life of passion while expanding your comfort zones and growing as a person.

It was not easy to achieve my bucket list dream of walking the South West Coast Path, but I guess that if it was going to be easy, I would have done it years ago. I had to overcome my fear of doing things on my own, become more resilient and smash through some long-held limiting beliefs.

I achieved this by using a set of techniques that I have perfected over many years, such as prioritising and defining goals, breaking down big goals into step-by-step plans, and reflecting on progress made. I am sharing these techniques in detail to help you achieve your bucket list dreams, and in doing so, expand your own horizons.

I have been perfecting this process my whole life. It works for me, and I know that it will work for you too. Are you ready for a big adventure? If so, don't put it off; the time to act is now! Read on to take the first step towards your first milestone – deciding which dream to pursue.

Milestone One:

Ignite Your Dream

Waymarker 1:

Define Your Dream

'Life punishes the vague wish and rewards the specific ask. If you want confusion and heartache, ask vague questions. If you want uncommon clarity and results, ask uncommonly clear questions.'

—— Tim Ferriss, entrepreneur and author, in his book Tribe of Mentors

Your big adventure starts here! Follow the steps to this way-marker to prioritise the dreams on your bucket list, decide which dream to pursue and define it clearly. This is the start of your journey. It is time to buckle up for an incredible ride!

My Journey

When I decided that it was time to give up my desk job and daily commute, I knew that I wanted to do something more active and adventurous. Ideas for adventures flooded into my head as butterflies took flight in my stomach. Sailing around the world, dancing in Cuba, walking England's South West Coast Path, motorcycling the length of Chile, taiko drumming in Japan and cycling around the Baltic Sea have all been on my bucket list for almost as long as I can remember, along with many other things.

Long ago, I realised that I would not be able to do everything that I want to; life is just too short. I had an ever-expanding bucket list and an ever-shrinking amount of time left. I had a choice. I could do nothing, prioritise my list, or pick something at random. Doing nothing was not an option that I wanted to consider, and I did not like the idea of picking something at random. If I prioritised my list, I could tackle the most attractive or time-critical item first.

I started by filtering the list against a few deal-breakers.

I knew that having an early success would spur me on, so I wanted to complete my first adventure within a year. I also did not want to be away from my husband for too long. I was not going to squander our relationship in exchange for adventure. Leaving Mike for more than a few weeks did not seem right or fair.

So, I filtered out the items that did not meet these requirements. They remain on my list to consider next time – this filter was only for *this* adventure.

Some things on my list were similar to each other, and it made sense to tackle one of those before the others. There is a piece of piano music called *Journey to Nidaros* that Alexander Chapman Campbell wrote as he walked St Olav's Way from Oslo to Trondheim. Whenever I hear it, the music instantly transports me to Norway. I can feel the warmth of the sun on my face and see the hills rolling away to the horizon ahead of me. I can hear my feet crunching on the gravel of the path as I walk and the birds singing as I wake in my tent. I imagine talking to other pilgrims, although they are few and far between and most do not speak English. I now have a strong desire to walk the same route, so it features prominently on my bucket list.

Back in my twenties, I had a similar reaction to reading a book called *500 Mile Walkies* about a man who walked the South West Coast Path. I had wanted to walk the path ever since.

As I live in the UK and had never hiked or camped on my own before, it seemed sensible to walk the South West Coast Path before tackling St Olav's Way. Doing that would develop my backpacking confidence in a country I was familiar with. St Olav's Way could wait for another year.

The next step was to identify other criteria that were important to me and score each option against them. I considered how excited I was by the idea, how much I would grow as a person, how much adventure I would have, whether there were any options to have a positive social impact and the level of environmental impact associated with doing each item.

We are so privileged to live on such a beautiful planet that is full of wonderful people. I do not want to harm either as I tick things off my bucket list. And if I can have a positive impact while I do those things, then all the better.

Of all my bucket list dreams, walking the South West Coast Path won hands down. As well as the adventure and physical challenge, I could also talk to people about protecting our oceans and raise money for a good cause. I chose one of my favourite charities, the Marine Conservation Society.

I imagined strolling along the clifftops, admiring the view and drinking in the fresh sea air day after day, pleased at last to be achieving my long-held dream. I would breathe in tune with the gentle pulse of waves breaking on the shore. I would talk to people as I walked, collecting donations and stories. I would see dolphins, seals and basking sharks. I would eat seafood, freshly caught that day and full of flavour. I would collect more stories as I stayed in interesting places. It would take almost two months, but my husband would be able to join me for a few days here and there, and I would be able to complete the walk within the next six months. I would return rejuvenated and refreshed, bursting with life and full of stories to share. In short, I was pretty excited by the idea.

If your bucket list is longer than a couple of items and you try to progress everything at once, you will not be able to give any of those things the energy and focus that it needs. You are more likely to feel overwhelmed and far less likely to succeed. Filtering and prioritising your bucket list allows you to focus on your most compelling dream and start your journey.

Now it was time to define my challenge more clearly. I was going to walk England's South West Coast Path in June and July 2020.

I would walk by myself, although I would be open to other people joining me for sections of the path. I would stay in places with beds rather than carrying a tent. I would talk to people about the importance of protecting our oceans, and I would raise £10,000 for the Marine Conservation Society. Walking 630 miles would be a stretch, and raising that much money would be challenging, but neither was impossible. The idea excited me and met all the requirements I had identified during the filtering and prioritising process.

Of course, things did not quite turn out like that — they never do — but I had at least decided which dream to pursue and defined it clearly.

Defining your dream well gives you clarity over what you are trying to achieve. The SMART model can help with this:

Specific

It can be difficult to plan for vague dreams. For example, I could have defined my dream as 'to walk a long-distance footpath'. That might mean five miles or five hundred. It might mean all in one go, or over the next 20 years. It is far too vague to turn into any sort of meaningful plan.

You can make the definition of your dream more specific by considering the five W's – what you want to do, who will be involved, where you will do it, when you will do it and why you want to do it.

Measurable

How will you know when you have achieved your goal?

You can break down larger goals into stages to measure progress as you go along, rather than just at completion. This will help you to check whether you are heading in the right direction or need to make a course correction. This process is covered in Waymarker 4.

One thing that I think is particularly important to understand is that measuring success should be on your own terms. Living your bucket list is about doing something for yourself, not to please someone else. Some purists think that walking the South West Coast Path means following the line of the path exactly. In some places, I deviated from the path because the route was not clear. In others, I had to walk inland because I was at risk of being blown off the cliffs. Those purists would say that I did not complete the path. I don't care what they think! I walked from one end of the path to the other, following it as closely as I sensibly could. I was walking to achieve my dream, not theirs, and was successful on my own terms. This is not the time to do things because other people think that you should, but because you think you should.

Attainable

I recommend that you start by choosing a dream that is achievable within a few months. This will give you an early win that will encourage you to tackle more challenging dreams in the future. If you do choose a BHAG (a big, hairy, audacious goal) that will take years to achieve, you can always break it down into smaller SMART goals so that you can see yourself making progress.

Relevant

Your dream needs to align with your values – it needs to matter to you. If you have filtered and prioritised your dream effectively, you can be confident that it already meets this criterion.

Timely

An ambitious but realistic deadline for completing your dream will help you to maintain focus and motivation.

Your Journey, Step-by-Step

Step 1: Create your bucket list

a) Create a list

Put on your favourite music, set a timer for 15-30 minutes and write down all your bucket list dreams. Think about all the things you have always wanted to do or would love to do someday. Continue writing until the timer goes off. You might find it useful to grab some coloured pens and create a mind map (see diagram below), as this can help to release your creativity. Do not worry too much about whether you have captured absolutely everything — this is not a one-off process. You can add to your bucket list at any time.

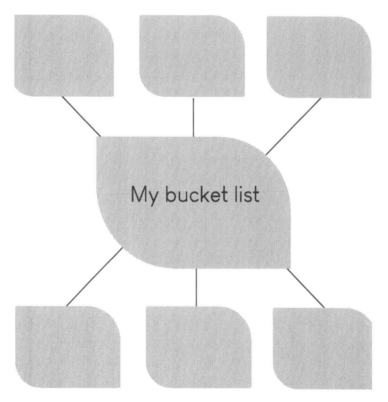

Step 2: Filter your list

a) Group and order

Group similar dreams together and determine whether these naturally fall into an order of progression.

For example, walking England's South West Coast Path and Norway's St Olav's Way were both on my list. It made sense to me to practise closer to home, so I chose to walk the South West Coast Path first.

b) Consider combinations

For example, if you have always wanted to learn to paint and always wanted to visit Paris, you might be able to find a painting course in Paris and tick two things off your list at once.

c) Identify your deal-breakers

These are the lines that you will not cross. For me, I had to be able to achieve my dream within 6 months to a year and did not want to be away from my husband for too long. Your deal-breakers will be different, and they will probably change over time.

d) Filter your list

Filter your list against your deal-breakers. Consider carefully. If you are creative, you might be able to find a way to achieve your dream without crossing those boundaries. For example, if your dream requires you to be away from your family for too long, it might be possible for them to join you for some of it or for you to split the trip and spend some time at home in the middle.

Step 3: Prioritise your list

a) Identify criteria

Determine which criteria you want to score your dreams against. Think about and list your values and any long-term objectives you have.

b) Consider timescales

Identify any dreams that have absolute timescales and therefore need to be prioritised. For example, it is becoming less safe and less feasible to walk to the North Pole every year because there is less sea ice. It would be sensible to prioritise that dream over others if it was on your list.

c) Score against your criteria

For every dream, give a score of one to five for each criterion with five being the best. Total the scores to determine which dream to focus on. You might find it useful to create a table, either by hand in your journal or on a spreadsheet, to document this stage.

As always with scoring mechanisms, it is important to check that the result passes the 'makes sense test'. Does pursuing this option first make sense to you? Imagine working towards your dream and how life will be once you have achieved it. How will you feel? What will you see, hear, smell and taste? Are you still excited? Is this vision enough to see you through some tough times, when your resolve could waver?

Step 4: Define your dream clearly using the SMART model

Is it specific, measurable, attainable, relevant and timely?

Review

You have reached the 'Define Your Dream' waymarker if you have:

- Documented your bucket list.

- Filtered your list.
- Prioritised your list.
- Decided which dream to pursue.
- Defined that dream using the SMART model.

If you have taken all these steps, then you have done some great work and are ready to move on to the next waymarker. Congratulations! Take a moment to pat yourself on the back. You have started your journey towards living your bucket list.

Try doing this physically – lift one arm above your head, then drop your hand down to the middle of your shoulder blades. Pat yourself three times. I bet you are smiling now — it is hard not to when you are doing this!

If you have not finished all these steps, then please do complete them before moving on to the next waymarker. I don't want you getting lost on the mountain!

I hope that you have had some fun thinking about your dreams like this and that you are excited to move on to the next step. It is normal to be a little nervous at this stage too. After all, if you are going to grow while achieving your dreams, you are bound to feel a bit of discomfort.

I was certainly nervous when I started on my journey — I had never done anything like this on my own before. But I was also excited to find out how it would unfold.

Reaching the next couple of waymarkers will help you to ensure that your excitement overrules your nerves. Read on for the next step!

Waymarker 2:

Smash Your Stumbling Blocks

'Believe you can and you're halfway there.'

— Theodore Roosevelt, 26th President of the United States

Now that you have defined your dream, it might be tempting to dive straight into doing it. However, if it was that easy, would it still be on your bucket list? Reasons for not pursuing your dreams can easily stack up and stop you in your tracks, even if you have the best intentions. So in this chapter, we will explore some of the things that might make you stumble and see how many of them you can either smash or sidestep.

My Journey

There were plenty of reasons why I had not turned my dream into reality in the past. The most significant of these were my limiting beliefs – false beliefs that have constrained me.

One of the biggest has been drummed into me since I was a little girl. It is this: if you are female, it is not safe to be out in the world on your own, especially after dark or where help is not at hand.

'My dad will walk you home.'

'Call a taxi – it's not safe to walk on your own.'

'Call me when you get there to let me know you've arrived safely.'

The messenger always seems to have your best interests at heart, but appearances can be deceiving. It is not in your best interests to take so many precautions that you miss out on life.

If you are told something enough times, you start to believe it. Even a bolshy feminist like me, working hard to smash down unfair barriers, can get caught out. So, over the years, I developed a belief that walking alone in the countryside is not safe for women. Sometimes, I was conscious of this and pushed the boundaries, starting to walk more on my own as I moved into middle age.

Even in my home town of Malvern, which must be one of the safest places in the world, I listened intently and checked behind me as I left the built-up area. I was keen to spot anyone following me into the 'danger zone', especially when I walked at dusk or in the dark. My heart thumping in my chest, I would continue, determined not to let my fear rule my life. That was my rebellion; walking on my own near my home, where it was relatively safe.

A lot of this limiting belief was deep in my subconscious. I did not even consider the option of walking long distances on my own or camping without a companion. I had never found someone else to walk the South West Coast Path with, so I had never done it.

Even after I identified that I had this limiting belief and was trying to fight it, another one surfaced and joined it. Having always walked and camped with other people, I was not sure that I could do it on my own. What if something went wrong and I needed help? How would I fare with no one else to bounce ideas off?

Now, I was battling against two limiting beliefs. But at least they had shown themselves, which gave me a fighting chance of beating them.

I looked for statistics on how many women are attacked while walking in the countryside in the UK. Very few. I put myself in the shoes of a man who wanted to attack women and thought about where I would wait to find a victim. A lonely path in the middle of nowhere with very little passing traffic was not at the top of my list! I found women on Facebook who hike and camp on their own, and have done for years without incident. I was beginning to feel more confident.

I considered the practicalities of other situations where I might need assistance. Hiking England's South West Coast Path is not like being in the wilds of Alaska. I would never be very far from other people or shops, so I would be able to get help if I needed it.

I could always call a taxi and spend a night in a hotel if necessary. Mike's words rang in my head. 'Is anyone going to die?'

On the South West Coast Path, as long as I did not fall off a cliff, the worst thing that was likely to happen was a minor injury or the discomfort of being cold or wet. Having put a few contingency plans in place in case I needed them, I felt more confident again.

To build my confidence further, I picked the brains of friends who are long-distance walkers, joined relevant Facebook groups and asked questions in our local outdoor equipment shop.

And I practised. First, I walked to build my fitness. Then, I hiked with a pack. I tried out my equipment so that I was confident to use it. I camped on my own in a safe space with my car nearby. Then, I wild camped on my own, without my car but still close to home. I smashed each of those stumbling blocks one step at a time.

Reasons for not pursuing our dreams can easily mount. Some might be real, but many will be limiting beliefs — false beliefs that constrain you. Limiting beliefs do not serve you in pursuing a life of passion. They might include things like not being good enough or needing to have a certain amount of money. You might think that people like you do not or cannot do things like this.

Once they have been identified, many stumbling blocks can be smashed using logic, learning or practice, shrunk by creating contingency plans or creatively sidestepped.

You are unlikely to achieve a long-held dream without a degree of discomfort. Those barriers that keep us feeling secure and comfortable can also act as walls, blocking our personal growth. Are you committed to breaking through them?

I am terrified of failure, perhaps as a result of another limiting belief about what failure is. I am embarrassed to admit that I have sometimes sabotaged the chances of success by not really trying properly. For some bizarre reason, it feels OK to fail if I have not really tried. But if I try my best and fail, then I am a failure. This is, of course, utter nonsense, but nevertheless a trait that I sometimes see in myself.

My head knows that the biggest failure is to not give yourself a proper chance to succeed. Even so, my heart needs to be constantly reminded that any failure is one step closer to success. Sometimes in the last thirty years, it has felt better to have an unfulfilled dream than to risk 'failing'.

Most successful people 'fail' time and time again. They learn from each experience and grow. This is not failure — it is the path to success. It is only failure if you do not learn from the experience.

And then, there was the classic excuse – that I did not have time to walk the path. It takes weeks to complete a 630-mile walk, but rather than just believing this assumption, I could have queried it. Some options do not involve blocking two months out of your diary. Some people walk the path a week at a time. If I had used one week's leave from work a year, it would have taken me seven or eight years to complete the path. This means that I could have completed it almost four times in the time it took me to do it once. Or I could have walked the Wales Coast Path too.

Another option to reduce the time commitment would have been to run it – the fastest runners take around ten days to complete the path. If I had considered this as an option, I could have completed it in just two weeks' annual leave.

My heart sinks when I think about this. If only I had focussed on my dream more closely, I could have achieved so much more, so much sooner. Please do not let the same thing happen to you.

> Assuming that you will not have the time (or money) to complete your bucket list challenge might be creating an unnecessary barrier to your success. There may be creative ways to progress that make both manageable. This is covered in more detail in Waymarkers 8 and 9.

Your Journey, Step-by-Step

Step 5: Smash your stumbling blocks

a) Identify potential stumbling blocks

Give yourself 10-15 minutes, put on some background music and list all the reasons you can think of why you have not already pursued your dream. Repeat the process for any additional reasons you can think of for not pursuing your dream now. And repeat again to identify any limiting beliefs you might have. I find mind maps useful for this step because colours and drawing help to boost my creativity.

Here are some prompts that you might find useful:

- What limiting beliefs do you have that might stop you from achieving your dream? E.g. You are too old, not good enough, female, disabled, not educated, can't afford it.
- What do you fear if you pursue your dream?

More will probably come to mind later, but this will give you a start. You can always add to the list as you progress through this process. In fact, the process will probably prove to be iterative — back and forth, adjusting as you go.

b) Avoid stumbling

For each of the stumbling blocks you have listed, think about how you can smash or sidestep them using logic, learning and practice.

- Logic — How valid is the reason/belief? Research the reality, find out whether anyone else like you has ever done it before. If the belief is valid, can you sidestep it?
- Learning — how can you learn from other people's experience?
- Practice — is there a way that you can practise in an environment that feels safe until you gain confidence?

Review

You have reached the 'Smash Your Stumbling Blocks' waymarker if you have:

- Identified the reasons why you have not yet achieved this dream.
- Identified the things that might stop you from achieving this dream now.
- Identified any relevant limiting beliefs.
- Identified any fears that are holding you back.
- Worked out a strategy for smashing through all those stumbling blocks.

If you have done all these things, then congratulations! Take a moment to reflect on what you have learnt and give yourself a drumroll for taking such an important step forward. (Use a table if you don't have any drums.)

If you have not finished all these steps, then please do complete them before moving on to the next waymarker. If time and money are two stumbling blocks that you feel will be hard to smash, then do not worry — these are tackled specifically in Waymarkers 8 and 9.

Now that you have started to clear your route forward by identifying and smashing potential stumbling blocks, it is a good time to clarify and strengthen your reason for wanting to pursue this dream. This will give you a strong sense of 'why', which will help you to see this project through.

3

Waymarker 3:

Make a Decision – and Mean It

'Know your why and fly, girl, fly.'

— Jamie Kern Lima, entrepreneur and co-founder of IT
Cosmetics

I enjoy walking and I love spending time by the sea. I was en-
chanted by Mark Wallington's book *500 Mile Walkies* when
I read it way back in my twenties. After reading it, I often talked
about walking the South West Coast Path, but somehow, I never
quite got round to it.

I started it once, walking for a long weekend. The sun
warmed my face, the sound of the waves soothed my soul, and

my heart trilled when I saw a flick of hares frolicking in a field. It was a superb weekend, but it was not the start of a journey as I had hoped. I did not just return home after that weekend, I also returned to my comfortable 'I've always wanted to do that' state.

So, what was it that changed, that turned my dream into reality after 25 years of procrastination?

The simple answer is that my reason why became stronger, and when your 'why' is strong enough, you will decide to act.

This chapter will help you to understand your 'why', strengthen it and give you the ammunition you need to make a decision that sticks.

My Journey

I have felt the age of 59 looming for some time now. That is the age at which my mum contracted ovarian cancer and died in a matter of weeks. My dad is a healthy octogenarian, which often leaves me wondering whether his genes or my mum's are stronger.

My life changed irrevocably after my mum died. I realised that I should not wait until I retired to start enjoying myself. I left my now ex-husband, who put all his energy into his work, leaving nothing for me. I became self-employed, started to love my work, and tasted success. But I did not walk the South West Coast Path.

Every now and again, the little voice in my head chirped up. 'You say that you want to walk the South West Coast Path, but you don't really. You hate long-distance walking. Your hips and knees will hurt. You'll get cold and wet. It will be miserable.'

All these thoughts stemmed from an experience I had when I was 21. It was so unpleasant that I can still remember it vividly all these years later.

My friend and I decided that we would walk the Wolds Way to blow away any mental cobwebs before our final exams at university. We did not have much money at the time, so we bought a guidebook and generally made do with the kit we already had. I did need a new waterproof jacket, which I bought a few days before we set off, along with some fuel for our stove.

The weather was dreary all week. It often rained, and I found that my new jacket was not waterproof, so I spent the week cold and wet. The fuel we had bought for the stove did not work properly. We could not get water to boil, which meant that none of our dehydrated food cooked properly. There was no chance of some cheer from a nice cup of tea or a hot meal. Our tent and sleeping bags were heavy, and our packs did not fit well. My shoulders were covered in painful red welts. My hips ached so badly that I dreaded stopping for breaks and having to warm them up again afterwards. In short, it was a thoroughly miserable week, and I swore that I would never go on a long-distance walk again.

So, even though *500 Mile Walkies* made me want to walk the South West Coast Path, that desire did not outweigh my fear of another experience like the Wolds Way.

Everything we do is driven by a desire to move towards pleasure or away from pain. The stronger of the two pulls is usually to avoid pain. Understanding what is driving you, whether it is pleasure, pain or both, gives you a good foundation to launch from.

Everyone understands something of the pleasure associated with their bucket list dreams, or they would not be dreams in the first place. That pleasure is often not enough on its own. Understanding the pain that you associate with moving towards those dreams is the first step towards reducing its influence. This could be fear of failure, fear about what could go wrong, or something else entirely. Fear can, of course, be a good thing, alerting you to real dangers. But it can also stop you from taking calculated risks if you let it.

When I turned 50, 59 loomed even larger. The fear of dying without achieving my dreams grew. But even that was not enough. I needed one final push. This came from a consultant who had conducted a series of breathing and blood tests on me while trying to diagnose a cough that had floored me for months. When he told me that it was whooping cough, I sighed with relief. There would be no long-term implications and I was already well on the mend.

I was feeling light as a feather as I picked up my coat to leave. I was going to be fine. As I reached the door, I made a throwaway comment about an existing condition that he had unearthed while doing all the tests.

'And things will just carry on the way they have always been with my small lungs, I guess.'

'Oh no, having that condition means that you are more susceptible to respiratory disease as you get older.'

My life changed at that moment. My mood switched from light as a feather to heavy as a lead balloon in a heartbeat. My horizons came hurtling towards me as my brain translated his words. 'If you want to have adventures, you had better do it now, while you can.'

Not being one who stays down for long, I soon rallied. This was the nudge I had been waiting for. It was time to shake things up a bit and there was no time to waste.

I already strongly associated pleasure with the idea of walking the South West Coast Path. Evidently, this was not enough on its own to overcome my fear of the pain of walking. My reasons for not walking the path stacked up: I had a deeply unpleasant experience of walking a long-distance footpath when I was younger; my hips were aching all the time; my knees were painful when I did too much exercise; I would have to find almost two months to walk in; etc., etc., etc.

Now, on the other side of the scales, I had the added pain of NOT pursuing my dream. If I became incapacitated at an early age and could no longer walk the path, I would be sorely disappointed in myself. Suddenly, the scales were tipped in favour of me going.

It does not necessarily have to be an external factor that drives the change. Understanding the strongest drivers for you and visualising how you will feel if you do and do not achieve your dream can strengthen your resolve without any external factors changing at all.

Once you have done this, you should have a strong reason why you want to achieve your dream. If you have not got a strong 'why' at this point, then perhaps this is not the right dream to pursue after all.

Once I had made my decision, I wanted to commit fully. I contacted the Marine Conservation Society, met with them and told them my plans. I set up my crowdfunding page (www.crowdfunder.co.uk/julias-jellyfish-journey) and asked my family and friends to donate. Now that I had made my plans public, I had to forge ahead. After 25 years, the time for procrastination was over.

The final thing to do before you start planning is to make a decision. That might sound odd, but I mean a real decision — one that you have fully committed to. The rewards for pursuing your dreams can be immense, but it is rare to achieve immense success without immense effort. Are you willing to move ahead and commit to the process?

If your 'why' is strong enough, then making a decision becomes easy and failure is not an option. However, there is no harm in reinforcing that decision. They say that the most effective way of conquering an island is to burn your boats. The way that I tend to do this is to go public. I tell friends and family what I am doing. I announce it on Facebook. On this occasion, I also told the Marine Conservation Society what I was planning and started fundraising. For me, that means that there is no going back. I have a reputation to uphold — if I say that I am going to do something, I do it.

A few years ago, when I decided to run a half-marathon (another bucket list dream), I asked a friend to run with me and we entered a race together. That meant that I had a deadline, and I had to train, or I would be letting both of us down.

What will you do to reinforce your decision?

Your Journey, Step-by-Step

Step 6: Commit to your dream

Follow this step to help you fully commit to pursuing your dream.

a) List the reasons FOR

Start with a blank sheet of paper and draw a line down the middle, from top to bottom. On the left side of the page, under the heading FOR, write a list of all the reasons you can think of to pursue your dream. For each of these, draw an arrow whose size is relative to the strength of that reason, pointing towards the centre line. Remember to include the pain associated with NOT pursuing your dream as well as the pleasure associated with pursuing it.

b) List the reasons AGAINST

On the right side of the page, under the heading AGAINST, write a list of all the reasons you can think of NOT to pursue your dream. This time, draw your arrows pointing left. Remember that where you have developed strategies to deal with stumbling blocks, those arrows should be smaller than they would have been if the stumbling block remains on the list at all.

Your list should look something like this:

FOR		AGAINST
Reason 1 ⟫⟫	⟪	Reason 1
Reason 2 ⟫⟫	⟨	Reason 2
Reason 3 ⟫⟫⟫	⟪⟪	Reason 3
Reason 4 ⟫⟫		

Download a template for this step from: www.juliags.com/liveyourbucketlist

Completing this step will provide you with a clear illustration of how strong your 'whys' are, compared to your 'why-nots'. This part of the process will help with the logical element of decision-making.

However, it is also important to bring our emotions into play to make a decision that sticks. This is where the next step comes in.

c) Imagine how you will feel when you have achieved your dream

Bring the answers to these questions alive in your imagination.

- Who or what will you be grateful for, for helping you along the way?

- Who will you have helped, and how does that make you feel? What do those people look like when you have helped them?
- What skills will you have developed? How does that make you feel?
- What challenges will you have overcome? How does that make you feel?
- While you are living your dream, where are you? What can you see, smell, hear, feel and taste?

Once you have imagined these things vividly, write them down or draw them. This will help to crystallise those positive thoughts in your brain.

d) Imagine how you will feel if you do not pursue your dream

The next step is to imagine how you will feel in a year, 5 years, 10 years and 20 years if you have not done absolutely everything you can to achieve your dream:

- How will you feel about yourself?
- How will your life be, compared to today? What can you see, smell, hear, feel, taste?
- How does that compare to the life you have already imagined?

Again, once you have imagined these alternative futures, write them down or draw them.

Completing this step will either give you a strong reason why you want to achieve your dream or help you to realise that actually, this thing that you thought was a dream is not really that important to you after all. If you find that you cannot fully commit to a decision, that is fine — it is always better to work these things out sooner rather than later. Return to Waymarker 1 and revisit your choice of dream or Waymarker 2 to smash through some more perceived stumbling blocks.

e) Go public

Tell your friends, declare your intentions on social media, start fundraising or join an event. Create some peer pressure for yourself to continue down the path you intend to.

Review

You have reached the 'Make a Decision and Mean It' waymarker if you have:

- Considered your reasons for pursuing your dream — and not doing so.
- Imagined how great you will feel when you have achieved your dream.
- Imagined how bad you will feel if you do not try to achieve your dream.
- Ignited passion for your dream.
- Made a positive decision to pursue your dream.
- Gone public with your decision.

If you have done all these things, then you are making excellent progress. Not only have you reached this waymarker, but you have also reached the 'Ignite your Dream' milestone. Take a moment to reflect on what you have learnt and congratulate yourself for getting this far. Would a celebratory dance make you smile?

If you have not finished all these steps, then please do complete them before moving on to the next waymarker.

You will notice that I have not talked about the practicalities of achieving your dream yet; that will come later.

So, you have defined your dream, you have smashed some of your stumbling blocks and you have considered your 'whys'. You have made a decision to pursue your dream, and you have committed to that decision. The next step is to start planning.

Milestone Two:

Make a Plan

Waymarker 4:

Break Down Your Journey into Stages

'One step at a time is all it takes to get you there.'

— Emily Dickinson, poet

I expect that your excitement is mounting now. Your journey is almost underway – you know where you are going, you have smashed some potential barriers and made a firm decision to continue. Before you just dive in and set off, you need to work out how to get there.

Following this process helps to ensure that you get everything done in the right order.

To reach this waymarker, you will break down your journey into stages and then individual steps, in the order in which you need to do them. This will make the journey to achieving your dream far more manageable.

My Journey

I should have been reclining on the clifftop, drinking in the view of the sun setting over the shimmering ocean. Instead, I was striding out, my heart palpitating wildly, hoping that the light would last just a little bit longer. It was the first night I was camping on the path, it was about to get dark, and I had not yet found somewhere to pitch my tent. I paused for a moment, closed my eyes and breathed deeply until my heart calmed into its usual rhythm, albeit slightly fast.

I told myself that my tent was small, that I was bound to be able to find somewhere soon. I reminded myself that I had a plan for this situation. I retrieved my head torch from my rucksack while it was still light enough to see what I was doing and continued my search.

Relief flooded through me when I spotted the tent-sized patch of grass just as dusk was settling into night. Five minutes later, as I tightened the final guy rope, the last of the sunlight disappeared, replaced by inky darkness. There was no artificial light here, except for a few blinking buoys out to sea and an oil tanker gliding by in the distance.

Wind back six months, and I would never have thought that I would have the guts to do this. Back then, I had never even camped at a campsite on my own, let alone on a clifftop, miles from anywhere.

I had planned to stay in hotels and similar during my adventure, but the coronavirus pandemic had changed that. As soon as lockdown restrictions were eased, England's South West filled up completely with tourists. There were more visitors and fewer beds than normal, which meant that I could not guarantee I would find somewhere to stay. Even campsites, many of which were working at reduced capacity, were so full that they could not accept any new bookings.

Plans need to be flexible to allow for changing circumstances. My initial plans involved staying in hotels and similar every night of the walk. When that became unrealistic, I had a choice – either delay my dream for a year or find another way of doing it. I had already committed to completing the walk that year, so I found another way.

All sorts of things that are outside your control can happen to scupper even the best-laid plans. Because of this, you need to be prepared to revisit your plans if circumstances change.

So, with much trepidation, I updated my plans. I was going to have to camp, on my own, in the wild as well as at campsites. I was going to have to carry a heavy rucksack as well as walk 630 miles with an ascent equivalent to four times Mount Everest.

And I needed to revisit my existing kit, none of which was designed for such an ambitious trip.

Breaking down your journey into smaller stages will make it feel more manageable. One of my stages was to become walking fit. Another, added when my plans changed, was to gain confidence to wild camp on my own.

If you then break down each stage into individual steps, the whole journey will feel even more achievable. For example, to gain enough confidence to wild camp on my own, I first stayed in my tent with my husband, who is a more experienced camper than me. The second step was to camp somewhere that I knew well on my own, but with my car nearby so that I had a safe place to retreat to if I felt that I needed it. The third and final step was to wild camp on my own, on a trail that is near home so that my husband could rescue me if necessary.

When you start planning, it might not be possible to see the whole of the route. If that is the case, just plan 1-2 stages or steps ahead and keep adding to the plan as you progress. It is a bit like driving a car in the dark - you can never see the whole of the road ahead, but more is revealed as you progress.

So, I took baby steps. First, I invested in a lightweight tent and a warm sleeping bag.

Then, I practised camping in my new tent with my husband.

Sometime in the middle of the night, I was startled awake. Mike squeezed my hand – he had heard it too.

We were in a completely safe space — tucked into a glade in the small woodland that we own. So, when we had heard gunshots in the distance as we drifted off to sleep, we had known there was nothing to worry about. But that shot was close. Really close. Maybe right at the boundary of our woods.

My eyes flew open, straining to see, even though it was pitch black and I was in a tent. It was fear, not logic, that was driving me. I rolled over as quietly as I could and breathed into Mike's ear so that only he could hear.

'How close are they? Are they on the track? I think they are in our woods, on the path near the tent.'

We hunkered down, silently contemplating the best course of action. Bang! Another shot – even closer. Didn't they know that we were there? Hadn't they seen our car? The footsteps became clearer, following the line of the track, past our car and out of the woods. No more shots were fired once our car was in view. It was a poacher, then, not wanting to be caught.

Sure that the poacher had gone, our adrenaline levels finally dropped. Sleep slowly reclaimed us.

A little later, my eyes flew open for a second time, my heart thumping in my chest again. This time, it was a deep, throaty bark, really close to our tent, that had woken me. My brain told me that it was just a dog fox walking through the woods and that he would pass on by without causing us any trouble. But my primal instincts told me that that noise represented danger. I sat bolt upright, fully alert. He barked again. And again. He was not just walking through. He knew we were there, he had stopped. Did his barking signal aggression? Or confusion? Or was he just warning other foxes in the area of our presence? Fox attacks in the UK are rare, but not unheard of.

Mike clapped. Three loud, clear claps. One final bark and the fox moved on. I sat there, listening intently for long enough to be sure that he had gone, before lying down. Eventually, sleep wound its sultry arms around me. The next thing I knew, it was daylight, and I could hear the tantalising sizzle of breakfast cooking on the campfire.

I have no idea how I found the courage to stay in the woods on my own the next weekend, but I did. And having crossed that hurdle, it was not too big a stretch to walk a local trail that takes two days, and wild camp overnight.

The last rays of the setting sun lit up the field as I approached, inviting me to investigate. The grass was long and wet, but there was a flat area right next to the hedgerow. If I pitched my tent there, it would be out of sight of any casual observer and sheltered from the wind. The perfect wild camping spot had revealed itself to me at the perfect time.

As I pitched my tent, I had visions of marauding gangs of youths driving doughnuts around the field in the dark, spotting my tent in the corner and thinking that it was good game. I have obviously watched far too many of the wrong type of film!

To my surprise, as soon as I zipped up the door to my tent, I felt safe, warm and cosy. Listening to the reassuringly familiar sounds of owls hooting in the trees and badgers snuffling around the tent, it did not take long to fall asleep. Step-by-step, my plans were beginning to come together.

Some steps and stages might be linked. If so, it is helpful to place them in the correct order. For example, I had to be walking fit and relatively confident with my tent before I could walk the local trail to try wild camping.

Habits can be a relatively painless way of achieving some of your steps. For example, when I was training to walk the South West Coast Path, I went out walking every morning before I did anything else. Getting up and leaving the house with my walking kit became a habit. A great example of the value of a habit is cleaning your teeth. You are (most likely) in the habit of doing this every day. You do not need to use up any willpower to do it, or use any energy making a decision — you just do it.

One good way to start a new habit is to set reminders on your phone. Sometimes I also put a poster up in my house somewhere obvious to me and my husband and complete it daily. For example, at the moment, I have a picture of a thermometer on my fridge that I colour in every day with how many words of this book I have written against my plan.

Because it is so visible, Mike often asks me how I am doing. This is another great way to generate some peer pressure to support your journey.

Your Journey, Step-by-Step

Step 7: Plan your route

a) Create a timeline

Use a fresh sheet of paper or double-page spread in your journal, set up with one of the long sides at the top. Write today's date in the top left-hand corner and the date that you plan to achieve your dream in the top right-hand corner. Add time markers across the top of the page in appropriate-sized chunks — most likely weeks or months.

b) Create stages

Take a stack of sticky notes and start to break down your dream into separate stages. Each stage represents the completion of a mini-project on its own that will have individual steps within it. For now, just focus on the stages, not the individual steps. Write the name of the stage in the middle of the note and the approximate duration underneath, if you know it.

Include any of the actions that you identified to smash potential stumbling blocks in Waymarker 2.

c) Place the stages in your timeline

Once you have all your stages on sticky notes, think about what order you need or want to do them in. Are there any easy wins that you would like to start with? Are there any that need to be done before another starts? Write anything that needs to have been completed before you start in the top left-hand corner and anything that needs this stage to be complete before it can start in the bottom right-hand corner.

If you do not know what some of your stages are, just create one that says 'Work out what other stages I need'.

Place these stages in order and add them to your timeline with planned start and finish dates.

A simplified timeline for my South West Coast Path walk might have looked something like this:

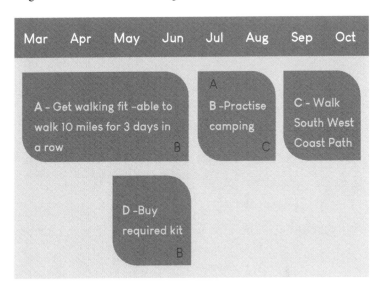

d) Sense-check your timeline

You now have an outline route map for pursuing your dream. Remember that your plan needs to be flexible — be prepared to revisit and revise it as you progress. Review it now against busy times at work, holidays or similar to make sure that you have not made any unrealistic commitments.

e) Create step-by-step plans

Now it is time to get into some of the detail. For each of the stages, create a list of steps that need to be taken and add start and finish dates to those steps as appropriate. If you do not know the detail yet, you can leave blanks and fill them in later.

f) Consider creating useful habits

Could any of these steps be turned into a useful habit? If so, write HABIT next to it, and when it is time to start that step, think about the best way for you to turn it into a habit — something that, after a while, you won't have to think about — you will just do it.

Download a free thermometer template for tracking progress with habits from: www.juliags.com/liveyourbucketlist

Review

You have reached the 'Break Down Your Journey into Stages' waymarker if you have:

- Created a timeline.
- Split the journey into separate stages and added these to your timeline.
- Sense-checked your timeline.
- Created step-by-step action plans for each stage.
- Considered how you can successfully turn some of those steps into habits.

If you have done all these things, then you deserve to give yourself a high five — you have the beginnings of a plan, a route map to achieving your bucket list dream. As with the pat on the back at Waymarker 1, try doing this physically. Raise one hand in front of you and jump as you bring the other up to it in a high clap. Any little celebration that makes you smile will subconsciously encourage you to continue.

Now take a moment to reflect on what you have learnt to get to this point.

If you have not finished all these steps, then please do complete them before moving on to the next waymarker.

You now know what you want to achieve, you have broken down your main dream into more manageable stages and broken these down further into the steps you need to take to complete each one.

You are ready to head to the next waymarker now. It will help you to add more detail to your plan and fill in some of the gaps.

Waymarker 5:

Do Not Reinvent the Wheel

'Plagiarism saves time.'

— JCI UK catchphrase, 2007

When I was an active member of JCI UK, an organisation that empowers young people to create positive change, this catchphrase was buzzing around. No-one was suggesting that members pass off someone else's work as their own, which is the strict definition of plagiarism. Rather, it was about learning from other people's experience and adopting proven successful strategies.

This phrase has stuck with me ever since. I am always looking for ways to save time by learning from other people's experience, and if you want to pursue your dreams, then I recommend that you do too.

My Journey

A crowd had congregated in the shower block, sharing horror stories about the last few hours' camping. The night had receded, but the storm had not. The wind was howling around the building and whisking through the hedgerows outside. We were right on the tip of Cornwall at the edge of the Atlantic Ocean and our campsite had taken the full brunt of the storm since the early hours of the morning. Storm Alex had arrived with gale-force winds that had combined with heavy rain to make for a dramatic night for camping. One couple's tent had failed completely. Drenched with rain, they had resorted to sleeping in their car.

I had walked into the campsite with a neighbour who had joined me for a few days. The warden had warned us about the storm, so we had tucked our tents in close to a Cornish hedge. These stone walls filled with earth and topped with shrubs make an excellent windbreak. The wall had sheltered us well, but even so, it had been a wild night. The wind had pushed the rain under the flysheet and into my neighbour's tent. Everything was damp. His clothes, his sleeping bag, everything. Which meant that his rucksack would be heavy that day, and he would have a cold night if we camped again.

Luckily for me, my husband Mike is an experienced camper, so I had copied what works well for him. After all, plagiarism saves time — learning from Mike's experience was far faster and more pleasant than having to learn the same lessons on my own. He had taught me how to pitch my tent to withstand a storm, and I had practised before I left home.

As the sun had set on the night of the storm, it lit up the horizon like a burnished gold band below unthreatening, fluffy grey clouds. It was hard to imagine that a storm was on its way. It was even harder to imagine a few hours later when we returned from the pub. A full moon was shining in a clear sky, its light reflecting off the calm sea. The air was still and stars were twinkling gently above us, where they were not obscured by the light of the moon. Everything was calm, peaceful and quiet.

Just in case the warden was right about the storm, I battened down the hatches. I checked that all my guy ropes were taut, that the pegs were secure, and that everything was packed into dry bags in case the tent leaked. I followed Mike's advice, step-by-step.

As I slept, I became aware of the wind whipping the tent and the rain thundering down on the flysheet inches above my head. I did a quick mental check. Was the tent still the right shape? Yes. Was I dry? Yes. I barely completed those thoughts before falling back into a deep sleep.

> Reinventing the wheel is time-consuming and can be deeply unpleasant. Learning from other people can help you to identify what works well and what does not without having to find out the hard way. In short, plagiarism saves time.

In the morning, I was woken by the light filtering into my tent. I was still warm and dry. I sat up and checked the rest of my belongings. All dry. Good! It was still stormy, so I did not want to venture out yet. I packed everything up into my rucksack, fitted its waterproof cover, pulled my waterproofs on and only then ventured out into the rain. With a cup of tea in hand, I dashed over to the shower block, where I stayed for the next hour or so, listening to tales of woe from other campers.

That afternoon, my neighbour had a look of grim determination on his face. 'Is it time for a tea break?' became a frequent refrain. The weight of his pack was causing him a great deal of pain and had clearly taken the joy out of the walk for him. Not only was he carrying damp, and therefore heavy, kit, but he had also packed kilos of stuff that he did not need. I had already learnt my lesson about carrying a heavy pack — not from my own experiences, but those of others.

My wonderful friend Hazel walked the Camino de Santiago de Compostela shortly after we met. It took her five weeks, and it was the first time I had known anyone who had walked that far. I was very impressed, partly because of the distance and partly because she had travelled on her own. She inspired me to start walking long distances and was happy to share some of her knowledge with me to make my experience as good as possible.

It was Hazel's voice that I heard playing in my head every time I stopped for a break, 'Remember to change your socks and air your feet.' And as I toyed with my packing list, 'How heavy is that? Do you really need it?' and 'Can you make your pack lighter?' Plenty of items were, quite rightly, jettisoned before I set off.

And then there was Maggie and Ian. It was late afternoon and I had had a hard day's walking. I had planned to Couchsurf that night, but their systems had crashed before I had got my host's details. I had three more miles to walk to the nearest campsite. I was tired, fed up and wondering about my sanity, plodding along with my head down, when I heard a jolly Scottish woman addressing me. 'How far are you walking?' And then, 'We live near the campsite, we'll show you a short cut.' Maggie and her husband Ian are also long-distance walkers. I gained a spring in my step and the next hour flew by as we walked, and talked.

One of the stories they told as we strode along was from when they hiked Scotland's West Highland Way. A group of lads had set off at a similar time to them, and every day, they noticed that the group was smaller as, one-by-one, the lads gave up. Finally, there was only one left. At the end of a punishing day's hike, he too decided that he had had enough. As he left the trail, he offered Maggie and Ian the food that he had not yet eaten. As he pulled it out of his rucksack, they were astonished to find that he had been carrying a lot of low-calorie, heavy food, including a bag of apples. No wonder they had all given up, carrying that much weight with them!

Maggie and Ian's advice to carry food with the highest calorie to weight ratio came rushing back to me when I asked my neighbour what he had in his rucksack to make it so heavy. One of his answers was a bag of apples from his garden!

You might find that existing friends and family can help you in your quest. They do not need to have completed exactly the same challenge as you. They could have some relevant experience to share if they have done something similar. My friend Hazel has never backpacked with her tent, but she has done a lot of long-distance walking. She was an excellent source of advice about the walking element of my trip. I found other people who are more experienced in camping, including my husband, to give me advice about that.

During the planning phase of my walk, I absorbed as much advice as I could from a range of sources. I referred to a guidebook to the trail for practical information. I joined a Facebook group for people walking the trail where members post inspiring photos of their walks, give advice about good camping spots, and answer all sorts of questions about hiking the path. And I frequently referred to the path's official website, which contains all sorts of useful information.

A trawl on the internet and social media may well turn up gems of advice. Look out for blogs or books to read, podcasts to listen to or social media groups to join. There may be training courses you could attend or clubs you could join to help you to learn and practise specific skills.

Learning from people who have been successful and what they did right can be very useful. Copy those actions that have worked for them and make sense to you. Equally, it can be useful to learn from those who have not been successful and what they did wrong. Avoid making the same mistakes yourself. The key here is to be able to tell the difference and not to copy the actions that caused someone to fail. Do not just believe things blindly – check the source, and sense-check the advice.

Your Journey, Step-by-Step

Step 8: Identify opportunities to learn from others

a) Look for opportunities

Take a look at each of the stages in your route map. Could there be any opportunities in there for you to learn from someone else, whether that is a friend, a family member or someone you do not know?

Be careful not to go down a rabbit hole of research! For each significant stage, set yourself a time limit of 15 minutes and a specific outcome to find out the most useful opportunities to learn from other people. List:

- All the people you know who might be able to help. Consider immediate family, close friends, colleagues, business contacts, your wider friendship circle and people who are members of the same club/s as you.

- The books you could read.
- The relevant blogs you have found. Save these in a separate folder in your browser favourites.
- Relevant groups on Facebook, LinkedIn and other social media platforms.
- Organisations you could join.
- Experts you could pay for advice.
- Podcasts you could listen to while washing up, doing the ironing or out for a run.

b) Prioritise your list

Once your 15 minutes is up, spend another 15 minutes prioritising your list:

- Number each item.
- Draw a grid that is 3 squares wide and 3 squares tall.
- Write 'time commitment' on the left, with 'low' next to the bottom square, 'medium' next to the middle square and 'high' next to the top square.
- Write 'likely value' along the bottom with 'low' next to the square on the left, 'medium' next to the middle square and 'high' next to the square on the right.
- Place the number of each item on the chart, depending on how much time they are likely to take and how much value you anticipate getting from taking that action.

Your grid should look something like this:

Time commitment

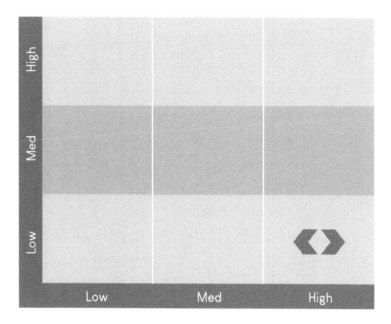

Likely value

Download a free template of this grid from:
www.juliags.com/liveyourbucketlist

c) Decide which actions to take

Choose the most relevant items from the bottom right-hand corner of the chart (high value, low time commitment) and add these to your route map. You might also want to consider the financial cost and how much you would enjoy each option when deciding which to choose.

Setting a timer is essential for this step – if you spend too long researching online, you could find yourself losing momentum.

Review

You have reached the 'Do Not Reinvent the Wheel' waymarker if you have:

- Identified opportunities to learn from others.
- Decided which of these opportunities you should pursue.
- Added them to your route map.

If you have done all these things, then congratulations – it is time to give yourself a treat – a cup of your favourite tea or slice of cake, perhaps. You have just saved yourself a load of time and increased your likelihood of success by learning from other people.

Now, reflect for a moment on what you have learnt to get to this point.

If you have not finished all these steps, then please do complete them before moving on to the next waymarker.

You have now taken two large strides towards completing your planning. You have an outline route map that you are beginning to fill in with stages and individual steps, and you have thought about how you can make the process more effective by learning from other people.

Earlier in the process, you worked out how to smash some potential stumbling blocks that are under your control. The next waymarker involves thinking about things that might go wrong that are outside of your control, and planning for these to a sensible extent. Read on for how to do this.

Waymarker 6:

Hope for the Best and Plan for the Worst

'Anticipating problems and figuring out how to solve them is actually the opposite of worrying: it's productive.'

— Chris Hadfield, astronaut, in his book *An Astronaut's Guide to Life on Earth*

If there is one thing you can be sure of, it is this: The path to achieving your dream will not be completely smooth. At some point, something will go wrong. It might be a little thing or a big thing, but it is massively unlikely that you will sail through the whole process without any bumps in the road at all.

This chapter is all about helping you to identify the things that are most likely to derail you and to have a plan in place to deal with them. Some people think that planning for a rainy day will make you enjoy sunny days less. I disagree. Planning for a rainy day can actually increase your enjoyment of sunny days. It will help you to realise that it might not stay like that forever, making you appreciate the sunshine more. And it will give you confidence knowing that you have a plan in place for when the clouds do arrive.

It will also increase your ability to deal with unexpected problems later in the process. Having solved one problem, you will subconsciously feel more able to solve another.

My Journey

I gradually awoke to the burgeoning light of dawn. The tinkling sound of splashing in the water trough next to my tent rose above the boom of the ocean crashing onto the shore below. Vertebra by vertebra, I sat up as silently as I could, not wanting to disturb whatever wildlife was there. One tooth at a time, I unzipped first the inner tent and then the flysheet. I peered through the tiny gap. Startled, a blackbird noisily took flight. Good morning world!

The previous day, things had not gone according to plan. But this morning, I could feel the thrill of having overcome adversity. More than that, it was a glorious morning. I turned around and unzipped the other door of my tent; the one facing the sea. The gentle breeze tickled my face as I gazed across the deep blue-green expanse to the horizon. What a place to start the day!

All sorts of things had gone wrong the previous day. I had not been able to find any accommodation and had arrived in the nearest village too late for dinner. I had been told that there was space to camp at the top of the beach, above the high-tide mark, but I could not see any suitable spot. I realised that I would have to camp on the clifftops instead, and heat up some of my emergency rations for dinner.

As I strode from the village to the clifftops beyond, the sun was setting over the sea. I took a couple of moments to enjoy the view, then hurried on. As the sky started to darken, I stopped and took my head torch out of my pack, ready to wear if I needed to. Ideally, I would find somewhere to camp while there was still some daylight, but if that was not possible, at least I could safely continue my search. And I had pitched my tent so many times now that I was confident that I could do it in the dark if necessary.

Luckily, I had planned for this contingency. I was carrying my tent, so I could camp if there were no beds available for the night. And if there were no campsites, I had practised wild camping, so I could find a spot alongside the path to pitch my tent. If I could not find anywhere to camp alongside the path, I could put my headtorch on and continue looking in the dark. And if there really was nowhere to camp, I could walk to the nearest village and take a taxi to a larger town inland, where there would be hotels with rooms.

In case there was nowhere to get food, I was carrying emergency rations – and a stove to cook them on.

Having all of these options available meant that, although my plans did not come together exactly as I had hoped, I was not derailed by the lack of somewhere to stay or eat.

> Having contingency plans in place can have positive effects, including reducing worry and aiding enjoyment.

Another big risk associated with my hike was the coronavirus pandemic. I put contingency plans in place for all the associated risks that I could think of. I took precautions against catching Covid-19 — I used hand sanitiser every time I touched something, wore a face mask while inside, kept my distance from other people and aired the room when staying in hotels and similar. I could not remove the risk completely, but I felt that by taking these actions, I had reduced it to an acceptable level. Coronavirus was here to stay, and we had to learn to live with it. We could not hide away for the next ten years waiting for a vaccine. But my planning did not end there.

If a full lockdown was imposed while I was away, if I was told to isolate through the government's track and trace system or if I caught the disease, Mike was on standby to race down to collect me and take me home.

If there was a partial lockdown and I was allowed to be away from home but pubs and cafés had to close, it would become harder to charge my phone. I was using my phone to take photos, write my diary and occasionally, navigate. So, I carried spare battery packs and a notebook and pen, just in case. I also carried a stove so that I would be able to cook meals, or at least reheat ready meals.

Having these plans in place did not make me more fearful of the pandemic. On the contrary, they were an essential part of my coping mechanism. They made it possible for me to continue with my plans despite the trying circumstances — and gave me the wonderful experience of camping on the clifftops, alone except for a solitary blackbird.

Planning for every minor bump in the road would not be feasible. By considering only those situations that are significant, either because they are most likely to happen or most catastrophic if they do, you can focus your attention where it is most needed.

Reducing the risk to a level that is acceptable to you will give you the confidence to continue with your challenge.

Back to that morning at the campsite with the wind whipping my tent and the rain hammering down on the flimsy canvas just inches above my head. I laid there snug, warm and dry in my sleeping bag, thankful that I had prepared for a storm before going to sleep.

My usual routine in the morning involved opening both the doors and allowing my sleeping bag to air in the breeze while I sat outside eating my breakfast and enjoying a cup of tea. Clearly, that would not be a sensible option this morning.

Instead, I instigated my rainy morning routine. First, breakfast in the lobby of my tent, careful not to spill any on my sleeping bag. Then, squeeze the air from my sleeping mat and put that inside my rucksack, creating a waterproof barrier just in case the rucksack cover failed. Then, squash my sleeping bag into its waterproof stuff sack and place that inside, followed by everything else.

At some point, I would have to leave the tent, but by then, all my kit would be safely inside dry bags and a rucksack with its waterproof cover in place. I would be wearing waterproof socks, trousers and jacket.

And it worked. I was proud of my planning. At that moment of adversity, I had not had to work out what to do. I had simply moved into autopilot, doing what was needed with minimal fuss. And it had meant that I enjoyed that day's walking far more for not being cold and damp, worrying about how to dry off my kit before it was next used.

My contingency plans included a mixture of working out how to respond to a given situation (e.g. rainy morning routine), practice (e.g. knowing that I could put my tent up in the dark if needed) and equipment (e.g. waterproof clothing, first aid kit, tent repair kit).

Working out contingency plans exercises the problem-solving part of your brain, and will increase your confidence to deal with unexpected issues when they arise.

Your Journey, Step-by-Step

Step 9: Identify significant risks

You have already considered internal factors. This time, consider what might change in the external world.

a) Identify contingency situations

Set yourself a time limit of 15 minutes and a specific outcome to list all the contingency situations you can think of that might impact on you achieving your dream. These could include:

- The weather.
- The political situation.
- Health – yours or others'.

b) Prioritise your list

Spend another 15 minutes prioritising your list, using the same method as you did for research:

- Number each item.
- Draw a grid that is 3 squares wide and 3 squares tall.
- Write 'Likelihood' on the left, with 'low' next to the bottom square, 'medium' next to the middle square and 'high' next to the top square.
- Write 'Potential consequences' along the bottom with 'minor' next to the square on the left, 'medium' next to the middle square and 'significant' next to the square on the right.
- Place the number of each contingency situation on the chart, depending on how likely it is to happen and what the consequences could be if it did.

This is what your grid should look like this time :

Likelihood

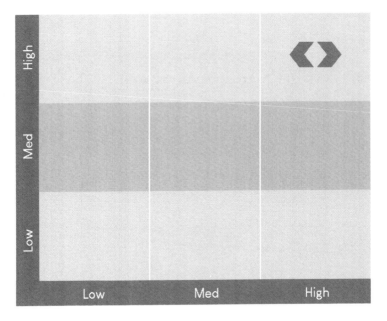

Potential consequences

Download a free template for this step from:
www.juliags.com/liveyourbucketlist

Step 10: Create contingency plans

a) Decide which contingency situations to plan for

This time, you need to focus your attention on those items towards the top right-hand corner of the grid – those that are most likely to happen and have significant consequences. For each of those contingency situations, write a list of actions that you need to take to reduce the risk to an acceptable level.

b) Document your contingency plans

Add these to your overall route map or keep a separate contingency plan, as appropriate.

If you are not sure about whether you have identified all the relevant risks, where to put something on your grid or what action to take to reduce the risk to an acceptable level, then add a step into your route map early on to do some research so that you can complete your contingency planning.

c) Keep the contingency plans up to date

As you progress through your project, if you think of something else that needs to be added to this list, please do so, and amend your plans as required.

It is essential during this process to use reliable sources of information for anything that you research. If not, you might find yourself missing key risks or taking actions that do not actually reduce them.

Review

You have reached the 'Hope for the Best and Plan for the Worst' waymarker if you have:

- Identified the most significant risks to you achieving your dream.
- Created contingency plans for those risks and documented them.

If you have done all these things, then you are progressing well. Give yourself a big thumbs up for taking the time to plan for things that might go wrong. Try doing this in front of a mirror. How many different happy or excited facial expressions can you make while doing this?

Then, take a few minutes to reflect on what you have learnt while progressing to this waymarker.

If you have not finished all these steps, then please do complete them before moving on to the next waymarker.

You have now defined your dream, worked out how to smash some of your internal roadblocks to achieving it and created a route map split into stages and step-by-step plans. You have considered how you can learn from other people and what contingency situations you need to plan for, and amended your route map accordingly.

The next thing to do before you set off on your journey is to think about how best to play to your strengths and manage your weaknesses.

Waymarker 7:

Use Your Superpowers and Sidestep Your Achilles Heels

'Who doesn't love doing what they are best at?'

— Julia Goodfellow-Smith

Now that you have a detailed route map in place, it is time to hone it before you set off. This chapter is all about fine-tuning your plan to make the most of your strengths and manage your weaknesses. This part of the process will increase the chances of you achieving your dream, as well as making the process far more enjoyable. After all, we tend to most enjoy doing things that we are good at.

My Journey

The first few days of my South West Coast Path adventure were a bit of a shock. After a long, hot summer, I rediscovered what it felt like to be cold.

I feel the cold more than anyone else I have ever met. My hands turn blue and my feet become numb at the slightest temperature drop. I chill quickly and heat up again slowly. I can be wearing multiple layers of warm clothing and still have goosebumps, while my husband Mike is perfectly comfortable in short sleeves.

But this summer had lulled me into a false sense of security. For months now, I had been warm. Occasionally, the weather cooled a little, but it never got cold.

I started walking the South West Coast Path at the beginning of September. The days were hot, but on those first few nights, the sky was clear and temperatures plummeted. Because of the coronavirus pandemic, most pubs were only serving food outside. In the evenings, we ate in their gardens. I layered up with all my clothes on and still shivered with the cold.

And I panicked. Why on earth was I starting this adventure in September? If I was struggling so much now, how would I survive the cold when camping in October? This was the first time — of many — on the walk that I had to give myself a stern talking-to. I would never live it down if I ducked out now; I would just have to find a way to manage.

I tucked an extra fleece into my rucksack and steeled myself for whatever lay ahead.

Towards the end of the walk, into October, I was delighted to find that I was still camping. I did sometimes feel the chill of autumnal weather, but only for short periods. I was thankful that I had the right kit with me – warm waterproof gloves, waterproof and windproof clothing, and best of all, a warm sleeping bag. I had packed a stove so that I could always have a hot drink if I needed it and cook myself a warm meal. In other words, I had used my superpower of planning to work around my Achilles heel of feeling the cold.

Feeling the cold is one of my Achilles heels that I always need to consider when I am planning anything. If I had not considered that weakness and worked around it, I would never have been able to achieve my dream.

What are your Achilles heels that you will need to manage to achieve your dream?

I identified another Achilles heel during the planning phase too. I had no experience of camping on my own or taking responsibility for camping activity. My husband is very experienced and competent, so in the decade or so since we met, I have been happy for him to take the lead when we have been camping. This means that I have never had to take any real responsibility on our camping trips. This weakness is not something that I could work around – it was one that I needed to address. I did so by seeking advice and practising, first with my husband and then alone, as you have already read. Once again, it was my planning superpower that I used to overcome another Achilles heel.

> There was no way that I could achieve my dream in the timescales I wanted to without addressing some of my weaknesses, such as lack of experience and confidence camping on my own. In fact, I am delighted that I did. I so loved camping on the clifftops on my own, I will be doing far more of it in the future now that I am confident to do so.
>
> Identifying and addressing your Achilles heels could bring you great benefits too. Which weaknesses do you need to address?

Until recently, I had never really thought of planning as being a superpower. It is just one of the things that I do. When you do something without any real conscious thought, it is easy to assume that those skills are used by everyone just as readily. It was only when my husband Mike commented on my planning skills that I realised that there was something special about what I do.

In the period before leaving for my walking adventure, I had tremendous fun both planning and completing each of my pre-walk stages. I drew mind maps in the shape of jellyfish, thought about what skills I would need, trained near home by walking on the Malvern Hills, practised camping on my own, and picked the brains of everyone I knew who could help.

All this preparation did not mean that the walk progressed exactly as planned — life is not like that — but it did mean that

I enjoyed the challenge far more than I would have done if I had been fire-fighting all the way around.

Just a few days into my walk, I set off in the morning into thick, wet fog, which remained through most of the day. The wind blew constantly, gusting up the cliffs, rattling my waterproof jacket and pushing me inland. At times, I could barely follow the path, bending my legs to lower my centre of gravity so that I could walk straight ahead.

Still, I loved the feeling of those first few miles. The steep slopes were punishing and my pack felt heavy, but I was walking well. I realised that I could manage the physical challenge — my confidence was building with every step.

Finally, the fog lifted enough to me to be able to make out the town of Weymouth in the distance. The cliffs lowered and the path dropped down to the beach. I thought it was going to be easy from here, walking along the flat seafront to Ferry Bridge, where I would turn inland to my campsite. I was wrong. This was the hardest part of the day by far.

The large pebbles on the beach were hard work to walk over, shifting in random directions under every step. As soon as there was a hard surface to walk on, I scuttled over to it. I was walking fast, thinking that I was almost there. As I approached the town, I realised that my feet were wet. They had probably been wet all day, but because the wind had been drying my legs out, I had not noticed. Big mistake!

I sat on the sea wall and aired my feet until they were dry — what a great excuse for a rest. I switched into waterproof socks and hurried on through the crowds and the sickly-sweet aromas of candyfloss and ice cream. Within seconds, the balls of both feet were hot. Foolishly, thinking that I was nearly there, I continued walking. It was only a couple of miles later that I stopped to tackle the issue. By this time, the mildly uncomfortable heat had become searing pain that was making me hobble. I was cursing – I knew perfectly well that you should stop as soon as you feel a hot spot developing.

Carrying on just gives blisters time to develop, and develop they had. I peeled off my socks, and there they were; two large blisters, each one deep in the pad of my foot near my toes. I plastered over them and squashed some hikers' wool into my socks to ease the pressure. I winced as I stood up again, but there was nothing for it; I had to continue. I still had a couple of miles to walk and did not want to fall at the first hurdle.

Walking along the old railway line out of Weymouth and then along the front of Portland Harbour should have been a joy. Instead, an agonizing lance of pain accompanied every step. An hour later, I arrived at my campsite and changed into flip flops. I was hoping for bliss, but alas, it was too late. I had two large blisters, one on each foot, and they were going to hurt now whatever I did.

That evening, I rested, but I still had 14 miles to walk the next day. It might have been sensible to rest for a couple of days while the blisters healed, but that would have felt like an early failure.

Luckily, I had a plan in place for if I got blisters. I plastered over them so that there would be no rubbing directly on the skin, applied hikers' wool between the plasters and my socks and gingerly set off. My feet were not comfortable, but I could walk without hobbling as long as I was careful about how I placed my feet. I was confident that my blisters were not going to get any worse. In the morning, I walked on smooth surfaces whenever I could because that was less painful. By the afternoon, my feet were beginning to recover, and I could walk on stony paths without wincing. My plan had worked, and although my feet remained sore for a few days, I had successfully turned what could have been a major delay into nothing more than a bit of pain that subsided quickly.

I employed my other superpowers that day too – positivity, courage and determination!

Identifying your superpowers and Achilles heels has great value. It means that you can put the former to good use and work out how to manage the latter, to increase your chances of success and your enjoyment of the process.

Your Journey, Step-by-Step

Step 11: Identify the skills or traits that you need to achieve your dream

a) List the skills and traits needed

Take a fresh sheet of paper or page in your journal and draw two lines, from top to bottom, to create three columns. The first is for the skills and traits that you will need, the second for a score and the third for notes.

Set your timer for 10-15 minutes, play some music, and, on the left-hand side, list all the skills and traits that you need to complete each of the stages in your route map, leaving some space between them. Use all the time, even if you think you have finished, as thoughts will often take a little while to surface. Use a mind map for this process and then add each skill and trait to the list afterwards, if it will help you to identify more.

Download a free template for your mind map from:
www.juliags.com/liveyourbucketlist

If you do not know which skills you need, add a research action into your route map early on. (If you wait until the start of that stage, you might find that it takes longer than planned to complete all the steps.)

b) Score yourself against the list

In the middle column, give yourself a score from 1-5 for each of those skills and traits, with 1 being something that you are unfamiliar with or not competent in and 5 being something that you are competent and confident in.

c) Plan to close the gap

In the right-hand column, add your notes. How can you turn your score into a 4 or a 5? This can be done by reorganising that stage so that you do not need that trait or skill, by developing your skills to close the gap, or by delegating to someone else who is competent in that area. (Even if you are pursuing your dream on your own, you might know someone who would be willing to help you.)

Step 12: Identify your superpowers and think about how you could use these more to achieve your dream

a) Map your superpowers

This is an ideal time to use a mind map. Draw a symbol in the centre that you relate to superpowers – the Superman or Superwoman symbol, perhaps, and build it from there. What do you love doing? What are you good at? What do you find easy? Think about times when things have gone well, and what you have done to support that outcome. It is a good time to ask other people who are close to you for input here. Your friends and family are likely to have some great insights to share with you, as my husband did for me.

Download a free mind map template from:

www.juliags.com/liveyourbucketlist

b) Use your superpowers

Looking at these superpowers, is there any way in which you can use them to achieve your dream? If you can, then you are likely to accelerate your progress and thoroughly enjoy the process.

Step 13: Identify your Achilles heels

Follow a similar process to Step 12. It might be hard to hear, but again, friends and family may be able to give you some valuable insights. Your weaknesses are likely to be things that you hate doing, put off doing, or make you anxious to think about doing them. Think about times when things have not gone as well as you had hoped, and what you did that affected that less-than-perfect outcome.

Looking at these weaknesses, could any of them trip you up on your journey? If so, is there a way that you can avoid it, re-design the task to reduce the risk, ask someone else to provide support in that area? Or is it something that you need to address to achieve success?

Step 14: Update your route map

The final step is to take all these things you have learnt and update your route map if you need to.

Review

You have reached the 'Use Your Superpowers and Sidestep Your Achilles Heels' waymarker if you have:

- Identified the skills or traits that you need to achieve your dream.
- Assessed your competence in those areas.
- Planned to close the gap.
- Identified your superpowers and how you can use them to your best advantage.
- Identified any Achilles heels you have and how to either sidestep or manage them.
- Updated your route map.

If you have done all these things, well done! Give yourself a moment of celebration – you are almost ready to set off on your journey. Stand in a superhero pose — feet apart, shoulders back and hands on your hips. Research indicates that taking up similar poses for just two minutes make people feel more powerful and reduce stress.

Before you move on to the next waymarker, think for a moment about what you have learnt about your superpowers and Achilles heels.

If you have not finished all these steps, then please do complete them before moving on to the next waymarker.

You are almost at the starting line now — there are just a couple of barriers you might need to address before setting off. If you do not have a way to find the time or money to follow your plan, then your dream will remain just that – a dream. The next waymarker covers time, and the following one, money.

Waymarker 8:

Find the Time You Need

'Time is a created thing. To say, "I don't have time," is like saying, "I don't want to."'

— Lao Tzu, ancient Chinese philosopher

You are almost ready to set off on your journey. You have defined your dream and created and fine-tuned your route map. You have boosted your plan by using your superpowers and managing your Achilles heels. The final thing to do before departing is to consider how you will find the time and money to follow your plan. This waymarker considers time, and the next, money.

My Journey

I had been lying awake for a while, thinking about what lay ahead that day. Sunlight was filtering through the curtains, dancing on my eyelids. A blackbird was perched nearby, its melodic singing competing with the rest of the dawn chorus. My alarm cut through the still air, telling me that it was time to get up. I smiled, a frisson of excitement reverberating through my body as I thought about what was going to happen before I started work.

The coronavirus lockdown meant that I was no longer commuting. As I needed to get fit for my big adventure, I had replaced the commute with a walk in the woods overlooking Malvern. It felt liberating to walk past the train station and on up the hill. The hike up the steep road was hard work, but the rewards were significant.

Every morning, we were welcomed by vibrant flashes of yellow as a flock of goldfinches foraged in the bushes around the path, just as we left the town. A small wooden post stands at the side of the path where the gently burbling stream is whisked away underground. Most days, a little robin perched on the post, its chest a rosy red, singing as we passed.

Every day, we heard woodpeckers tapping in the trees, foraging in the bark for breakfast.

As we followed the track up through the wooded valley, the soundscape changed. The traffic noise disappeared completely. All that was left in the silence was birdsong and the tinkling of the stream over its cobbled base. The nature of the air changed too; under the trees, it was cooler, fresher. It smelt of leaves and soil, not the cars, cooking and laundry of town. It was like walking into another world.

One day, a green woodpecker arced through the trees, flashing its yellow rump as it flew. It landed on a moss-covered trunk, and as if by magic, it totally disappeared. The camouflage of its feathers exactly matched the moss on the tree. I had never seen anything like it.

One of the trees was slowly decaying. Over time, I watched the bracket fungi on its trunk grow in size and multiply in number until there was layer upon layer of creamy-white mushrooms cascading down the tree.

Further along, the path opens out from the trees onto a grassy knoll overlooking the town. The valley is often misty in the morning. Scattered church spires pierce the thin white gauze overlaying the landscape. And the golden sun rises above it all, bringing the promise of a bright new day.

The coronavirus pandemic lockdown had created the time in my day that I needed to start my training. Instead of sitting on a train for an hour in the morning, I walked on the hills for the same length of time. Most days, Mike joined me. It was a magical time that set us up ready for whatever else we had to contend with, but that is not why we chose the morning. We chose this time because we knew that if we waited until later in the day, other things might have taken priority – a report that needed to be finished, or an urgent issue that needed to be resolved. We could only guarantee that we would go out for a walk if we did so first thing in the morning.

We all have the same amount of time at our disposal each day, week, month and year. What matters is how we use it. I chose to use the time I gained from not commuting to help me achieve my dream. If we are dedicated enough to pursuing our dreams, we will be able to find a way to give them the time they deserve. How could you use your time better to achieve your bucket list dream?

Ultimately, I resigned from my job and gave my full attention to achieving my dream, but there were many different factors in play. It is perfectly possible to achieve a lot of dreams while working too – or possibly even as part of your job.

As I was walking the path, when my feet were still a little sore from the blisters, I sensed someone walking behind me. I had already gone as far as I had intended that day but had not yet found somewhere to camp, so I was striding out, looking for somewhere to pitch my tent. I glanced backwards and saw that it was another backpacker, slowly catching me up. I stopped so that we could talk. From that point, we walked together for about three hours.

I was lucky enough to have bumped into Arthur (Artie), who is a legend on the path. Not because he looks rather like Michael Palin, although he does, but because he has now completed the trail so many times.

'I first discovered the path in the 1980's, and have walked it most years since. At first, I had to split it into two halves – I walked the first half one year and finished it off the next, because I could only take two weeks off work at a time.. I retired ten years ago, and have continued to walk the path every year since then. Sometimes I carry my tent, but this year, I am driving my tent between campsites and doing day walks with a light pack.'

We walked fast and hard together, but Arthur's company and conversation put a spring in my step. As we talked, he provided me with an excellent reminder that where there is a will, there is a way. It would have been easy for him to dismiss walking the path because he only had a few weeks of leave from work each year. Instead, he worked out how he could fit his dream into his holidays from work and achieved it over and over again.

Working out how much time you need to dedicate to achieving your dream is a useful exercise. This includes planning, preparation and execution. I had to find time to train, practise camping and complete the actual path. If I had not been able to walk the path in one go, I could have walked for longer each day and split it up into fortnights, as Arthur did.

Some of your stages might need consistent action and some might need concentrated action for a while — or you might be able to choose between the two options.

Once you know how much time you need, you can work out where you are going to get it from. It is not possible to magic additional hours into your day, so something else needs to give. In my case, I started by using my commuting time. Later, I sacrificed the amount of time spent in my woodland so that I could walk the distances I needed to. Arthur sacrificed the opportunity to spend his leave from work doing other things, like relaxing on a beach, so that he could enjoy walking the path time and again.

Your Journey, Step-by-Step

Step 15: Conduct a project time audit

For each of your stages, estimate the amount of time that will be needed to achieve it. Consider whether you will need to pay it regular daily/weekly attention, or whether it is better approached by setting aside a chunk of time in which to complete it.

You may not be able to estimate exactly, but this process should give you some idea of how much time you need to find to complete your project.

Include some contingency time in your calculations. I find that things almost always take longer than anticipated.

Step 16: Conduct a personal time audit

Create 7 sheets of paper, split into 24 hour-long sections.

For the next 7 days (or the last 7 days, if you are in a hurry to start and can do it), record how you spend your time in each of those hours. Include sleeping, food preparation, eating, working, socialising, travelling, exercising, watching television, and time spent on social media. Even if it does not take up a significant amount of any of your hour-long slots, check with Facebook and other platforms how many hours a day you are spending on them.

Download a free template for this step from: www.juliags.com/liveyourbucketlist

Step 17: Review your time requirement against your time audit

Think about all the parts of your day when you could carve out some time for your project.

a) Create a not-to-do list

What can you stop doing, without any negative consequences? For example, I found that, by not watching the news, I save around 45 minutes each day. I do occasionally check the headlines, but by and large, this has saved me a lot of time and improved my mood.

b) Combine activities

Consider whether you can combine any activities. For example, if you need to learn about something, you could listen to an audio book or podcast while exercising or doing the washing up. Sometimes, I combined training with socialising by walking with friends.

c) Swap out similar activities

Consider whether you can swap out similar activities. For example, if you enjoy watching films, it might help you to achieve your dream to watch films or documentaries about other people doing similar things.

d) Close the gap

Compare the time you have managed to carve out of your day, week or year to the time you need to achieve your dream. If there is a large time deficit still, consider revising your plans. Review the date by which you intend to achieve your dream, the steps you need to take, or where you are going to find the time from.

Step 18: Commit to carving out the time you need

Now that you have worked out how to find the time to complete your challenge, commit to it in writing. See Step 22.

Review

You have reached the 'Find the Time You Need' waymarker if you have:

- Conducted a project time audit.
- Conducted a personal time audit.
- Identified where you can carve the time you need out of your day, week or year.
- Committed to taking those actions.

If you have done all these things, congratulations! It is not always easy to find the time you need to achieve your dreams. Before you move on to the next waymarker, think for a moment about what you have learnt about your use of time, and congratulate yourself for identifying how you can carve out the time you need to achieve your dream.

If you have not finished all these steps, then please do complete them before moving on to the next waymarker.

Now, you have defined your dream, worked out a route map to achieve it, fine-tuned your plans, and carved out some time to pursue your dreams. Now, it is time to consider the final potentially significant hurdle - money.

Waymarker 9:

Find the Money You Need

'Anyone who lives within their means suffers from a lack of imagination.'

— Oscar Wilde, playwright

One of the biggest stories we tell ourselves, alongside that of not having the time to do something, is not having the money to do it. If money is no object to you achieving your dream, please feel free to skip this waymarker.

However, if you do not have unlimited funds and do not want to get into debt, then following the steps to this waymarker will help.

My Journey

Once upon a time, Mike and I lived in a big house with lots of space, lots of rooms and lots of staircases. We had a big mortgage to match the big house, with big monthly payments to match the big mortgage. One day, I found Mike in one of the spare bedrooms, sitting on the bed. 'What are you doing in here?' I asked, slightly confused.

He replied, 'I like to sit in all the rooms sometimes so that I feel like we're using the whole house.' That was the moment that I fully realised that we just did not need all that space.

A few months later, we decided to move to a different part of the country. When we talked about the type of house we were looking for, we realised that we would both be happy with something far smaller. A smaller mortgage would mean smaller monthly payments, even allowing for an earlier repayment date. So, we downsized, reduced our mortgage, and reduced our monthly outgoings.

Sometimes, we let out our spare bedroom to earn some additional income, which resulted in some interesting encounters with our guests.

We have a theatre near our house and had our room listed on the digs list for a while. One of our guests, a man called Carl, was an absolute hoot. He regaled us with hilarious tales from the theatre, and one day, decided to teach my very macho husband how to mince and exit a room by saying, 'Miss you, love you, mean it!' Cue a visit from our equally macho neighbour, who was somewhat surprised to find Mike and Carl both prancing around the house, wiggling their hips!

On one occasion, our theatre guest arrived with her partner and his young son, as arranged. His son rushed in and ran straight to our DVD collection. 'You're bound to have a DVD that Sophia is in!' And he was right, we did. We played with him on his Wii every day, and at the end of the week, we danced the night away with Sophia at the production's after-party.

Another of our theatre guests got a permanent job nearby and ended up staying as a Monday to Thursday lodger for a year, commuting back to his family every weekend.

We found, as planned, that with lower outgoings and the additional income from renting out our spare room, we did not have to chase income from work in the same way as we did before. This allowed us to chase some of our dreams instead. We spent some time working in Valencia, Mike studied for (and got) a PhD, and we bought a small woodland. We paid off our mortgage years earlier than we had expected to, just before the coronavirus pandemic hit. That meant that I could afford to take the time to achieve another of my dreams and walk the South West Coast Path.

> Unless money is no object, working out some sort of budget and financial plan will be crucial to achieving your dream.

I wanted to resign from work as soon as the Christmas break was over, but managed to stomach another two months of commuting before handing in my notice. This gave me some time to start planning, while still having an income. Even though I only had to give one months' notice, I worked for two more months. This gave me an additional month's salary, which almost paid for the trip by itself. As soon as I received that final salary payment, I put it into a new, separate bank account – my adventure account. Having struggled with my working life for months, I enjoyed working that final month, knowing that I would be spending the money that I was earning to achieve one of my dreams.

Once you know what the gap is between your available savings or income and what you need, you can start to look for ways to close that gap. That could be by reducing the cost of achieving your dream (e.g. wild camping instead of staying in hotels), making more money (e.g. working extra shifts or letting a room) or reducing outgoings (e.g. downsizing) to turn something that might seem impossible into something possible.

As the summer approached and it became clear that I would have to carry camping kit with me on my hike, I realised that I would need to buy quite a lot of new kit. Camping technology has come on in leaps and bounds over the last few years, making everything lighter. My new tent weighed only one-third of our old one. My existing sleeping bag had never kept me warm while camping, even in summer. The replacement is warmer and lighter. And I also needed cooking kit that was lightweight and reliable.

That all took what felt like a large chunk out of my adventure fund until I did the maths. I realised that if I camped for just 14 nights, everything would pay for itself in saved accommodation costs. And that was just for this trip. I camped for many more nights than that, so the change in plans actually resulted in a financial saving, although there was a greater upfront investment.

Having the level of financial freedom that we do also gave me more confidence to take on the challenge of the walk. I knew that, once the weather started to deteriorate as autumn progressed, I could afford to stay in a hotel rather than camping. And if I could not find anywhere nearby, I could pay for a taxi to take me to another town. When Storm Alex hit with winds so strong that I was actually blown off the path, I was glad that that option was available.

When we are at home, Mike and I meet every week for what we call our 'hot date'. We open a bottle of wine and review our finances. We always check our spend to date against our monthly budget and periodically check progress against our savings, investments and pension planning targets. We make decisions about where and when we want to invest and check up on progress against our action plans. The meeting does not always last for long but it does help us to keep on track financially.

As plans change, budgets and financial plans need to be reviewed and updated if necessary. A regular review of progress provides an opportunity to make adjustments as needed and stay on track.

Your Journey, Step-by-Step

Step 19: Create a project budget

a) Estimate the cost

For every stage, estimate the cost of each step. Consider:

- Direct costs. E.g. accommodation and meals while walking.
- Indirect costs. E.g. needing to take time off work that you don't get paid for.
- Equipment you might need to buy. E.g. a new tent, sleeping bag and cooking system.
- Insurance.
- Vaccinations and visas if you are travelling.
- Allow an additional amount for contingencies – costs you have forgotten to include, or that end up being higher than expected.

b) Create a chart

Create a chart that shows you how much money you need to complete each stage, including dates. For example, I needed to buy my new kit before I started walking, but I did not need to pay for accommodation until I had set off.

Your budget will not be exact at this stage – do some basic research about costs, but do not let the creation of your budget bog you down. It is perfectly alright to make educated guesses.

Download a free template for this step from:
www.juliags.com/liveyourbucketlist

c) Compare required funds to available funds

Work out what funds you already have available and how much you expect to have for the duration of your challenge. Add these numbers to the chart you have just created for your budget.

d) Calculate the gap

Work out the difference between the two numbers — what you are going to need and what you are likely to have — at each stage.

Step 20: Plan how to close the gap

a) Review your spending habits

Work through your last month's bank and credit card statements and split your expenditure into categories, e.g. groceries, utility bills, housing, going out. If you spend a lot of cash, you will need to work out what you spend that cash on, either by trying to remember or by keeping a tally for the next month.

b) Plan to close the gap

Be creative here – think of ways that you can:

- Reduce the cost of anything you have to pay for. For me, camping and wild camping both significantly reduced my outgoings. You might be able to complete your challenge as a 'mystery shopper', buy kit second hand or borrow it, or if you have a lot of social media followers, you might even be able to get a freebie in exchange for writing about your experience. If you have a birthday coming up, your family and friends might cover some of the costs as a gift.

- Increase your income. For us, we have rented out our spare room to Airbnb guests, a lodger and people who travel with theatre shows. And I worked for an extra month to pay for my trip. You might be able to work extra shifts, take on an extra job for a few hours a week or have a clear-out and sell the things that you no longer need. Local community groups are always on the look-out for speakers. Perhaps there is something you can already talk about, or you could talk about the experience of achieving your dream for a fee.

- Reduce your expenditure. Review each category on the monthly spending list you have just created and look for potential savings. Could you take a flask of coffee on the train, instead of buying a take-out? Could you switch your utility supplier to a company with a cheaper renewable energy tariff? Could you walk or cycle to work instead of taking your car? Could you even manage without your car?

Be as creative as you can. Remember, achieving your dream is at stake here.

c) Review your ideas

Create a spreadsheet or add to your chart how much you could close the gap by doing these things.

If this is not enough on its own to close the gap, consider whether you need some extra time to achieve what you want to. For example, an extra couple of months' worth of savings might provide exactly what you need, for just a small adjustment to your plans. Do not use this option lightly — it is not about kicking the project down the road, but actually doing it.

d) Create a financial action plan and monitor progress

This should contain everything you are going to do and the financial impact that will have. Refer back to it regularly to check on progress. I am a visual person, so like to create a visual representation of progress, whether that is a graph or something else. I often create a thermometer that I can colour in as I progress, and put it somewhere obvious like on my fridge door.

You might choose something that more closely represents what you are planning. On the left side, mark up gradations relating to the amount of money that you need to save. On the right side, mark up the dates by which you need to have saved that amount. And then, colour it in as you make progress. This provides an easy-reference way to see how you are doing against your plan, and will also encourage you every time you see it.

If you love spreadsheets, then you will probably already know how to do something similar with a graph.

Download a free thermometer template from: www.juliags.com/liveyourbucketlist

Step 21: Open a dedicated bank account

As you make and save money for this project, add it to the account straight away. That will make you far less likely to accidentally dip into these savings for other purposes and also help you to see how you are progressing.

Step 22: Commit in writing

Create yourself a certificate that states the following:

I, NAME, am committed to DREAM by DATE.

In order to pursue this dream, I am going to make time available by ACTION and the money available by ACTION.

Sign and date it, and put it somewhere visible as a daily reminder of what you are working towards.

Download a free certificate template from:

www.juliags.com/liveyourbucketlist

Review

You have reached the 'Find the Money You Need' waymarker if you have:

- Created a project budget.
- Compared required funds to available funds.
- Created a financial action plan to close the gap.
- Set up a system to monitor progress.
- Opened a dedicated bank account.
- Committed to your plans in writing.

If you have done all these things, that is a huge leap forward and it means that you have reached the 'Planning' milestone. Once you have reflected on what you have learnt about managing your finances, you are ready to set off on your journey! Stand in a victory pose for a couple of minutes, as if you were on a podium celebrating your success.

If you have not finished all these steps, then please do complete them before moving on to the next waymarker.

You have now smashed two potentially significant barriers to success – finding both the time and the money to be able to achieve your dream. Now it is time to set off. After all, planning is only of value if you put your plan into practice.

The remaining waymarkers will help to keep you on track as you progress. Bon voyage!

Milestone Three:

Achieve your Dream

Waymarker 10:

Give Yourself an Assisted Boost

'Come up with a mantra and say it to yourself a thousand times a day until it becomes real.'

— Rachel Hollis in her book *Girl, Wash Your Face*

Congratulations on starting your journey towards achieving your dream. Now that you have set off, here are a few tips about how you can give yourself a boost by using the power of self-talk and gifts from others.

My Journey

As I was nearing Clovelly in north Devon, I was subjected to a rather surprising attack.

I had been warned by some other walkers about the local shoot. Dead birds had rained down from the sky around them as they walked through this area. But it was not the risk of being shot that I had to contend with as I walked past. It was the game itself!

The path ahead was crowded with iridescent copper-coloured pheasants, the birds staying close to the edge of the woodland on my left. As I strode towards them, they squawked and flew a few metres to the side, as they usually do. Apart from one. I could just see it out of the corner of my eye, keeping pace with me. I stopped and turned towards it. It was about two metres to my right. It stopped and gazed fearlessly at me. I started walking again. It raced to keep up with me. When I stopped, it stopped. When I started again, it ran to keep up again. I was amused, so I videoed him.

I put my phone away, and when I went to step forward, realised that he was now at my feet, cooing at me. You do not often get this close to birds, so I calmly shot some more photos and another video, blithely unaware of what was going to happen next.

I took a step forward, expecting him to move out of my way. But he had other intentions. He stayed right where he was and started to peck at my boots. I thought that he was perhaps attracted by the shiny eyelets holding my laces, but then he started to fly up and peck at my legs too. I scurried forward briskly to try to lose him. Once again, he ran to catch up and continued to fly up and peck at my legs. I gently booted him away. Surely that would be enough to deter him. Oh no! He was back in a flash.

I picked up my pace as much as I could without tripping over him. He continued to follow closely, fly and peck. I shouted at him and waved my arms. I clapped. Nothing deterred him.

Through a gate into a woodland, he followed. Down some steps, he followed. I picked up a stick and tried to fight him off without hurting him. I ruffled the feathers of his neck and body with the stick, trying to push him away. I accidentally trod on his wing, at which point, I shrieked and he squawked. He was not deterred. He continued to follow and attack me. As I approached a flight of steps leading uphill, he dashed ahead of me and started to fly up in front of me. My heart was beating like an express train. How was I going to stop him from pecking at my face and seriously injuring me?

'Julia, you've got this.' It was the mantra I had been repeating to myself ever since setting off on my journey. I had adopted it from my husband, who had said it to me on multiple occasions before I started to walk on my own. If you hear something enough times, you start to believe it.

Adrenaline was throbbing through my veins, my heart pounding. I had a choice. I had to stop him, but he was not responding to gentle encouragement. I would have to seriously hurt him to stop him, and if I did that, I would have to kill him to be humane. That seemed like an altogether disproportionate response, so I took the alternative option and did what all brave adventurers would do. I ran!

I sprinted up those steps as fast as I could. He followed me. Through a gate, across a field and through the next gate, he followed. My rucksack was weighing me down and slowing me down. I was gasping for air, but I was gaining ground. Another couple of fields later, I dared to check behind me again. There was no sign of him. I slowed to a fast walk. At the next gate, I checked again. He had given up. Thank goodness!

I slowed right down and let my heart rate drop back to normal as the adrenaline slowly dissipated. It seems that my mantra was true. I could do this, even if it did mean running away sometimes.

There are parts of the South West Coast Path where the trail seems to just disappear over the edge of a cliff, or where steps are built into walls right above a precipitous drop. It is not a path for the faint-hearted. My mantra came in handy every single day to help me overcome my fear.

It also came in handy when I just needed a bit of encouragement.

The day that I pitched my tent under the arch of a rainbow had been a slog. Rain had lashed at us all day. Gales had continuously threatened to blow us off course. My walking companion had booked the last room in the village pub, and I had breezily said to him, 'That's fine, I'll find somewhere to camp,' while being just a little bit worried that I would not.

As he was shown to his room, I stood under the pub's canopy contemplating my options, reluctant to head back out into the maelstrom.

'Julia, you've got this.'

I turned to the man who was sharing the canopy with me, supping his pint.

'Excuse me, Sir, do you know of anywhere nearby that I might be able to camp tonight?'

He briefly looked up from his pint. 'No.'

It would not be light for much longer, and the cold was beginning to penetrate my layers of clothing. I needed to move, and I needed to find a spot for my tent fast.

'Excuse me, I hear that you are looking for somewhere to camp this evening.' The chef was sheltering just inside the kitchen door. 'There's a farmer a few hundred yards up the road who sometimes lets people camp in one of his fields.'

I could have hugged him! After a couple of false starts, I found the right farmhouse and they offered me the use of one of their fields.

The weather abated briefly, and as the sun set, a rainbow rose steeply over the field. The storm was due to worsen during the night, so I had to find a spot that was protected from the wind. There were no cows in the field at the time, but it was not long ago that they, too, had been sheltering from the storm. The grass in the only suitable corner was covered in wet, slimy cowpats. There was one cowpat-free area that was just big enough for my tent, so that is where I pitched it, repeating my mantra to myself.

'It's OK, Julia. You've got this.'

Self-talk is very powerful. When I was walking the South West Coast Path, I was good at keeping it positive to keep myself going. But occasionally, I found myself lapsing into negative self-talk, telling myself off for being so stupid or calling myself an idiot. I can honestly say that the latter approach has never helped to improve my mood or move me forward.

> Whichever story you tell yourself a lot is the one that you will believe, so it is best to make it a good one that serves you well.

That farmer had given me a gift by allowing me to camp in their field. Although there was a risk of sliding away on an avalanche of cowpats during the night, I knew that my tent was safe and that I could leave it to have dinner in the nearby pub.

In the 52 days it took me to hike the trail, all sorts of people showered me with gifts — total strangers like that farmer, as well as people that I knew.

Jane and Dave, who I met at a campsite, offered me a bed for the night as I passed their house. I did, of course, wonder whether they were axe-wielding murderers, but decided to trust them. They gave me a very welcome hot and powerful shower, a cosy night's sleep in a bed, delicious food and an evening of fabulous company.

Jo, who I worked with over 20 years ago, also gave me a wonderful meal, a bed for the night and some fantastic conversation as we walked together.

Although Jacqui is the sister of one of my school friends, I had not seen her for over 30 years. She and her husband were extraordinarily generous, giving me somewhere to stay for a few days as I passed their house.

Jacqui told me where to look out for a colony of seals at Godrevy Point a few weeks later on my journey. As I approached the point, I was feeling a bit battered. I had been slogging my way through Storm Alex for almost a week and there was no sign of it abating. I was constantly being blown around by the wind and had to battle for every step forward. The previous night I had camped, sheltered behind a pampas grass — a surprisingly effective windbreak — and I had planned to camp that night too, somewhere on the coast path. With the wind like this, my chances did not look good. So, I had my head down and was walking on autopilot when I remembered what Jacqui had told me about the seals.

I glanced down to the shore, not really expecting to see anything apart from the cold, grey waves pounding onto the rocks and sand. Could I see something swimming along the wave? I stopped to look properly. Yes! Two seals were hunting in the shallows, seemingly oblivious to the power of the waves slamming into the shore just metres away. That was better – I was now walking with a smile on my face.

It was hard work fighting my way around the headland in the wind, but far easier than it would have been if I had still been feeling blue. I noticed a low fence ahead of me at the edge of the cliffs. The sign on the fence was small and close to the ground, which made me curious. I stopped — and stooped — for a closer look.

'No sudden noises or movements.'

Another: 'Talk in whispers – do not shout.'

The roar of the wind and the thunder of the waves hitting the rocks below made these signs seem rather ridiculous. What could possibly be disturbed by people talking on the clifftops? I peered over the fence in fascination. What was going on?

There were lozenges, from creamy-white to deep grey, spread across the beach. A whole colony of seals! Some simply laid on the sand, resting. Some were bobbing in the water. As I watched, a large seal approached a mother and her calf on the beach. The mother reared up and a fight ensued until the interloper sloped away down the beach and into the sea.

At the far end of the bay, one of the seals was surfing. I can think of no other explanation. As it swam out to where the waves were breaking, it ducked its head down under the water. When it reached the edge of the breaker zone, it turned around and surfed back to the beach. Again and again. It did not appear to be hunting — I think it was just having fun. What a wonderful experience and a wonderful gift to have been given by Jacqui. If she had not told me about the seals there, I may well have just powered straight on past, nose down and eyes fixated on the path ahead.

Some of the gifts I was given, like these, were obvious. Some were disguised as something far more sinister, such as the incident with 'Angry Man' that happened close to the end of my journey.

I was pleased with the way my walk was progressing and, much to my surprise, I was still camping when I could, despite the cooler autumnal weather. That night, I was the only person camping at a holiday park. All the other residents were cosied up in caravans and campervans. I tucked my tent in close to some of the caravans as that was the only spot on the site that was sheltered from the wind. Once I had showered, I headed off to the bar for my dinner, where I could sit in the light and stay warm and dry for the evening.

A few minutes later, one of my campervanning neighbours rushed over to my table. 'Someone's trashing your tent.'

'What?'

'Someone's trashing your tent.'

I could barely believe it. Why would anyone do that? My first reaction was to head out and stop him, but the holiday park staff asked me not to. Their security guard was on his way, and my being there would potentially inflame the situation. I knew they were right, so reluctantly, I complied.

The bar staff rallied around me, while the warden, security guard and café manager went to deal with Angry Man.

My tent was indeed trashed. It was broken beyond immediate repair, apparently because he did not like how close I was to his caravan. I was carrying a tent repair kit, but it was designed to repair damage caused by storms, not people, and it was not up to the job.

The staff arranged for me to stay in a caravan in the neighbouring holiday park. They could not have been more helpful. The café manager bought me dinner in someone else's café, having lost my order in his own. The security guard offered me the use of his tent the following night if I still wanted to camp. He even offered to pitch it for me, so that it was ready for when I arrived.

The way that everyone reacted to the attack turned what could have been a tragedy into a triumph of human compassion. Angry Man's anger only played a bit part in the evening's proceedings — it was totally eclipsed by kindness on a grand scale. When the owner of the holiday park heard about the incident, he amplified that kindness even further by paying to repair my tent and making a generous donation to the Marine Conservation Society.

A couple of days later, as I walked up to Great Hangman, the highest point on the trail, I was musing about what had happened. Some of my friends had suggested that Mr Angry should be 'sorted out'. I love those friends and their concern for me but found myself disagreeing with their solution to the problem. I figured that it could not possibly have been me and my tent that made him so angry. There must have been something else going on in his life that was upsetting him. I remembered some of the characters I had met on my journey: Johnny, who had concluded that everything was love; Juli-La, who blesses both litter and the litterer as she picks it up; and Margot, who believes in the power of karma.

Inspired by their loving approaches to life, I sheltered behind the cairn at the top of the hill and sent blessings out in the wind. I willed the wind to reach Angry Man, for my blessings to swirl around him and delve inside him. I hoped that he would be able to reconcile his anger and find peace and happiness in his life. I hoped that the sun would shine on his face and that a gentle wind would be on his back, leading him to a better place.

I allowed my anger to be washed away by the wind. I let go of the fear that this incident had aroused in me, and arrived at a place of peace. It turns out that Angry Man gave me a gift with his attack. By pushing me, he made me more resilient. He reinforced my confidence in people wanting to help each other and reminded me about who I want to be. I could have let fear, hatred and vitriol fester inside me, but I realised that I would much rather be a person who sends blessings out into the wind and lives a life full of love, however weird that sounds.

There are gifts to be found in a wide variety of situations, as long as you are looking for them. Sometimes they are big gifts, like a night in a bed when you had expected to camp or a replacement tent when yours is trashed, but often they are small, like an encouraging 'hello' or being told where to find seals.

Sometimes, gifts are obviously gifts and a joy to receive. Sometimes they are disguised as something far less savoury, like having your tent trashed or having an unexpected problem to solve. For the latter, you might have to look quite hard to find the gift in the situation, but if you can, it is well worth the effort.

Your Journey, Step-by-Step

Step 23: Generate more positive self-talk

a) Identify existing positive stories

Make a note of some of the positive stories you tell yourself, or positive labels you give to yourself. These are the stories that serve you well, that help you to achieve what you want to in life. For example, I am determined, I am courageous.

b) Identify additional positive stories

What other positive stories can you think of? Think back to the work you did on superpowers for some inspiration.

c) Replace negative stories

On a loose sheet of paper, write down the negative stories that you tell yourself. For example, I am clumsy, I am always stupid. Are there times that you tell yourself off?

Think about what you would say to a good friend in a similar situation. Would you tell them off or be encouraging? Would you help them to focus on their strengths to overcome any negative thinking? Now write those positive thoughts in your journal, and discard the loose sheet of paper. You could have some fun with this, ripping it into shreds, screwing it up into a ball or burning it (please stay safe!) and mentally ridding yourself of those negative thoughts.

d) Strengthen your positive stories

Read all the positive stories you have written down. Cherish them, and strengthen them in your mind through repetition. Say them out loud to yourself — it really does work to help you believe them.

Set yourself a reminder to do this regularly, so that telling yourself positive stories becomes a habit.

Step 24: Look for gifts

a) Create a habit

Get into the habit of looking out for gifts from other people. Look specifically for gifts that will help you to stay on track with your journey or to enjoy it even more. Every day, take some time to think about what has happened that day, what people have said to you and how these could be construed as gifts.

When you come across a bump in the road of your journey, think about how that problem could be a gift in disguise as you solve it or work your way around it.

Review

You have reached the 'Give Yourself an Assisted Boost' waymarker if you have:

- Created a list of positive stories to tell yourself.
- Started to say these stories out loud to yourself.
- Started to create the habit of looking for gifts in every situation.

If you have done all these things, I hope that they have given you a boost. Having good habits of positive self-talk and looking for gifts in every situation can help to achieve your dreams and keep your motivation strong. Reflect for a moment about what you have learnt about yourself and what has changed on your journey so far and give yourself a standing ovation for telling such a powerful story.

You are now well into your journey of living your bucket list. You have a plan that you are implementing, and you have considered how you can boost your progress.

In the next chapter, we will explore some ways to make sure that you look after yourself, both mentally and physically, to complete your journey in good form.

Waymarker 11:

Look After Yourself

'An empty lantern provides no light. Self-care is the fuel that allows your light to shine brightly.'

— Unknown

On a long or difficult journey, it is essential that you take good care of yourself. In this chapter, we will be considering different aspects of your mental and physical health, as well as the balance of different elements of your life.

My Journey

The day that I walked with Mike's old school friend Phil, his sister Chris and her partner Nigel was one of my favourites on the whole path. The section of the coastline between Brixham and Dartmouth is beautiful. The landscape switches between woodland and grassland. Wild ponies nibble their way across the steep slopes leading from the plateau of the land down to the sea. There are numerous rocky inlets below the path with the emerald-green sea lapping against the shore.

This section of the trail is also one of the most arduous. The narrow path weaves around headlands, the land rising steeply upwards on one side and vertiginously downwards on the other. Like a rollercoaster, it rises onto the clifftops and back down to the shore, up and down steps and steep slopes over and over again.

Looking back at my photos from that day, it is beautiful, but no more so than other parts of the path. The beauty on its own does not explain why this was one of my favourite sections to walk. The explanation lies instead with the company I kept that day. All three of my companions lifted my spirits.

Nigel and Chris are people that funny things just seem to happen to. Take the sausage story as an example: Not long ago, they were at a restaurant. Chris had ordered a meal with vegetarian sausages, but when she took her first bite from one of them, she realised that the sausage was not vegetarian at all. Nigel called the waiter over. The waiter picked up the sausage, took a bite from it and put it back on Chris's plate.

'That is vegetarian, mate.'

'No, it's not. Can I talk to the chef, please?'

The waiter stomped into the kitchen and returned with the chef, both of them glowering. The chef picked up the same sausage, took another bite from it and replaced it on the plate.

'Yes, that is definitely vegetarian.'

By then, whether or not the sausage was vegetarian was irrelevant. Two members of staff had picked it up, taken a bite from it and returned it to Chris's plate, with no concern for hygiene at all!

They were so taken aback that Chris ate the rest of her breakfast, although she did choose to leave the by then half-eaten sausage.

Chris also had a good story to tell from her childhood. She accidentally invented foam parties on her last day at school by adding a large bottle of bubble bath to a fountain in the town centre. The thought of the town being overwhelmed by a tidal wave of foam, with her standing next to a police officer while surveying the scene still makes me giggle now.

Their stories kept me amused for hours. Sadly, some of them are rather explosive, and not repeatable!

And Phil was an absolute joy to walk with. Every five minutes, he would enthusiastically declare, 'Isn't that beautiful?' or, 'What a stunning view!'

All three of them find such joy in life, and in that stretch of coastline, their emotions rubbed off on me. They turned what could have been a hard day's walking into a thoroughly enjoyable one instead.

Conversely, because I was walking during the coronavirus pandemic, I was reading the news headlines every day so that I knew about any changes to the rules that might affect me. However, now and again, usually when I stayed in a hotel, I would make the mistake of watching the news on television.

And it was a mistake. I learnt that the news would fill me with dread and fear. It was right to be cautious at that time, but abject terror was not going to serve me well. To protect my positive state of mind, I decided that I would stick to the headlines, and investigate something in more depth only if I needed to. Negative emotions are just as catching as positive ones.

> Emotions are catching, whether positive and serving your best interests, or negative and damaging.

Despite enjoying the time I spent walking with other people, one of the things that has become obvious to me during the coronavirus pandemic and associated lockdowns is how much of an introvert I am.

Being an introvert does not mean that I want to be on my own. I am, in fact, quite sociable. It just means that it takes a lot of energy for me to be with other people and I recharge when I am on my own. So, in some respects, the coronavirus lockdown was a gift to me. It gave me time to recover from a year of working in an open-plan office when I was constantly with other people. It also gave me time to step back from my life of rushing to be here, there and everywhere.

I have realised that I need time by myself, in my own space.

Alison and I have been friends for almost all our lives, but I had not seen her sister Jacqui since I was at school. Despite this, as soon as Jacqui heard that I was walking past her house, she generously offered me somewhere to stay for a few nights. She and her husband Doug would drive me to and from the path each day.

I had arranged to call Jacqui when I reached Charlestown, an old port on the outskirts of St Austell. These days, it is no longer used for the transport of copper or china clay from nearby mines, but by tall ships and tourists. As I turned a corner on the approach to the harbour, I heard someone call out, 'There she is!' I looked up to see Jacqui, Doug and their dog walking towards me. The last thirty years melted away as we chatted happily through the rest of the afternoon and evening.

The next few days passed in a bit of a blur. Alison arrived, and we walked together for a couple of days, then Jacqui joined us for a few days. The hiking was great, the company was excellent, and it was wonderful to sleep in a comfortable bed every night.

For the last couple of nights of our time together, we stayed at a youth hostel because we had walked too far from their house for day trips.

Having been friends for so long, I am as relaxed with Alison as I am with almost anyone. I loved that she had taken leave from work to walk with me and appreciated the opportunity to spend a chunk of time with her. It had been a fun-filled few days.

Yet, on the last morning at the youth hostel, I hid under my duvet until I absolutely had to get up. I needed to give myself some space and time 'alone'. I valued the time that we had spent together, but I needed to recharge. I was looking forward to walking on my own and sleeping in my tent again, doing exactly what I wanted to do, in my own space.

My duvet time was enough of a recharge to have a fantastic day together walking to Lizard, the most southerly village on the British mainland. We chatted and laughed, and gawked at a huge seal that surfaced in a cove below us.

After a few grey days, the landscape seemed to have burst into colour. The spiky deep green of the gorse was punctuated by bright yellow flowers. Some of the heathers still glowed mauve. Even those that had gone to seed were a vibrant copper colour. The grey rocks were covered in a mosaic of white and orange lichen, and the sea was a rich azure.

As we neared the lighthouse and its enormous foghorns facing the path, I imagined how it would feel to walk past on a foggy day, with the deep boom not just audible, but reverberating through your whole body.

Doug unloaded my camping kit from the car and everyone waited patiently while I pitched my tent, before we headed off for an early fish and chip dinner. At the end of the evening, it was a bittersweet moment when we said goodbye. It had been such fun walking together and I would miss them, but I was also looking forward to walking on my own again.

The next day, the rugged Cornish coastline stretched out ahead of me. After a few days of blustery showers, the weather looked promising. The sky was a deep blue with just a few small fluffy clouds and a gentle breeze. I was back on my own. Despite my now heavy pack, I had the wind in my sails and I was walking well, with a spring in my step.

Introverts need to spend time alone to recharge. Conversely, extroverts need to spend time in company to recharge. Knowing where you are on the intro-/extrovert spectrum will help you to strike the right balance for your wellbeing.

I do not always want to be on my own. Another favourite moment on my journey was the day that I found my husband on a beach. I knew that he was on that stretch of path, walking towards me, but when I spotted the beach, I knew that he would not have resisted the temptation to stop.

I climbed down onto the pebbles, and there he was, perched on a massive boulder, gazing out to sea like a merman longing to return to the ocean. My heart skipped a beat as I walked towards him. He sensed me nearing and turned. Flippity-flop! My heart was thumping now, and my grin could not have been wider. We had known that it would be hard to be apart for the whole of my journey, so had arranged to spend some time together at the beginning, middle and end of the trail. And here he was – hurray!

Being aware of what is most important to you means that you will know what you need to protect while you are pursuing your dreams. In my case, Mike and I were both keen to ensure that our relationship was not neglected by being apart for too long.

Every day of my walk, I felt immense gratitude. I was grateful for having the opportunity to spend my days doing this, for being surrounded by such beauty, for good waterproofs when it was raining and for the sun when it was shining. On steep slopes, I was grateful that someone had built steps into them, even if those steps were thigh-high and incredibly difficult to climb. I was grateful for the heavy scent of ivy, which grounded me and made me feel at home, even though I was many miles away. I was grateful for having a tent that protected me from storms. And I was grateful for the birds that always appeared when I was feeling weary, seemingly singing to encourage me along. In short, I was tremendously happy with my lot, even though I was sometimes hungry, cold, tired and yearning for the comforts of home.

Practising gratitude is a great way to promote mental wellbeing. You do not have to wait for a big moment to come along to make you happy. Gratitude will feed your happiness from the smallest of everyday things.

The last hill of the trail was particularly hard. The path crosses Porlock Marsh before rising onto the cliffs one final time. In 1996, a storm breached the shingle ridge that separates the marsh from the sea. This means that the freshwater marsh has become salty where the seawater has penetrated. Most trees do not like having salty roots, so those that once stood tall and vibrant are now skeletons of dead wood, silhouetted against the sky. From a conservation perspective, this is an incredibly interesting and valuable landscape. For a weary walker slithering on muddy paths under a steely sky and heading towards a cliff shrouded in low cloud, it felt like sheer desolation.

The final climb onto the cliffs is short but steep. It felt like I was climbing a mountain at three thousand metres, rather than a hill only just above sea level. My feet were heavy. All I could hear was the rush of air in and out of my lungs. In and out; in and out. Every few steps, I had to stop to catch my breath. I was surprised that the sign at the bottom of the hill said that there were only 4.5 miles left to walk. I had thought that Minehead was further than that. The way that I was feeling, that was good news.

After slogging up the hill for a good thirty minutes but only covering a couple of hundred metres, there was another sign. Minehead five miles. I could have wept. But whatever the signs said, I knew that every step forward was a step closer to finishing, a step closer to triumph, a step closer to rest. So, I continued, one step at a time.

On the top of the cliffs, visibility was close to zero, and once I had brought my breathing back under control, there was total silence. The clouds were thick. I had no reference points to work to and the correct route was not clear. I could not see or hear the sea. Unusually, I had decided to walk this path without a compass – after all, all that I needed to do was to keep the sea on my left. 625 miles into a 630-mile walk, I started to doubt the wisdom of that decision. I pulled my phone out of my pocket, hoping that I had power and a signal. Great! I had both, which meant that I could pinpoint my position and direction of travel. I continued to pick my way across the cliffs in this fashion until the clouds lifted, just in time for me to see Mike and his old school friend, Phil, heading towards me.

I did not want to admit to Phil how exhausted I was; after all, on the day we had walked together a couple of months earlier, Nigel and Chris had recommended that I take a rest day once a week, and I had not heeded their advice. Mike had given me similar advice when I started training, and I had ignored him too.

I did not know it at the time, but my exhaustion was actually caused by severe iron-deficiency anaemia. I had realised that I had to be careful with my diet as I walked. I had intentionally chosen meals with a high-calorie content so that I did not lose too much weight, and I had made sure that I ate plenty of fruit and vegetables. The fact that my need for iron would intensify doing such endurance exercise had not even crossed my mind, and for that, I suffered.

It was sheer bloody-minded, dogged determination that got me through the final few days of the trail and up that last hill. I was not in great physical condition, but my mental state was excellent, aided, of course, by the good humour and uplifting company of Mike and Phil for the final couple of miles.

One way or another, looking after your mental and physical health while you are pursuing your dreams is essential. The last couple of weeks of my walk would have been far more enjoyable had I remained in good physical health. Luckily, I maintained good mental health, aided by the people I walked with.

Your Journey, Step-by-Step

Step 25: Wheel of health and happiness

a) Create the wheel

Draw a wheel with spokes leading out from the centre, labelled with the following:

- Healthy eating
- Fresh air/time in nature
- Exercise
- Rest
- Sleep
- Time spent with other people (if you are an extrovert) or time spent alone (if you are an introvert)
- Relationships (have more than one spoke for this if it is helpful)
- Self-confidence
- Any other things that you find important for your mental or physical health.

b) Mark your existing status on the wheel

Place an X on each of the spokes at the level at which you find yourself at the moment. The centre represents a low score (you are not satisfied with where you are) and the outside of the circle is a high score (you are totally satisfied with where you are).

c) Link the points

Draw a line from X to X around the wheel.

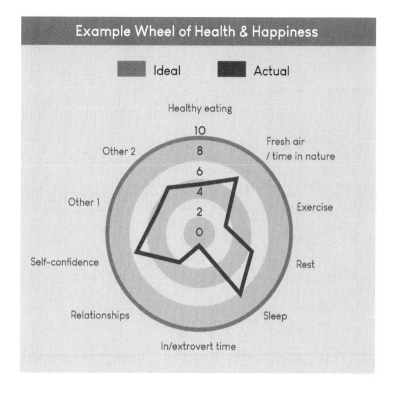

d) Review your wheel

Now imagine that this is a real wheel and you are trying to cycle with it. In an ideal world, all your Xs would be on the outside edge of the wheel and it would run smoothly. In reality, that rarely happens. Is there anything here that causes you concern? Do you need to pay some more attention to one element of your health, or is everything reasonably well balanced? Note any areas of concern and create a simple action plan to address those areas. This can be added to your overall route map if it is useful.

Step 26: Emotional audit

a) Create a table

Draw a line down the middle of the page of your journal, from top to bottom.

b) List emotion boosters

On the left-hand side, make a list of the activities and the people you spend time with that boost your emotions.

c) List emotion squashers

On the right-hand side, make a similar list, but this time of the activities and people you spend time with that upset you, make you doubt yourself or negatively affect your emotions in other ways.

d) Protect your emotions

Is there any way that you can spend more time with those activities and people on the left side? Can you reduce the amount of time with those activities and people on the right side? And if that is not possible, is there anything you can do to protect yourself from those negative emotions? For example, you might steer the conversation away from specific subjects.

Step 27: Gratitude practice

In your journal, make a note of three things that you are grateful for today. They could be little things or big things. Ideally, they are specific and have happened in the last 24 hours, but if you cannot think of anything, then cast further back in time.

Continue this practice daily if you need to create a gratitude habit.

Review

You have reached the 'Look After Yourself' waymarker if you have:

- Completed a wheel of health and happiness and addressed any concerns.
- Completed an emotional audit and considered how best to protect your emotions.
- Started a gratitude practice.

If you have done all these things, then your journey should become smoother and more enjoyable. Take some time to consider how far you have travelled and congratulate yourself before taking the next step. Is it time to relax in a lovely hot bath or hot tub?

You have most of the tools you need now to achieve your dream. But sometimes, there are huge external factors that can hit you like a storm and knock you off course. The next chapter will help you to think about how you can use the power of the storm to your advantage.

Waymarker 12:

Ride the Storm

'Why wait for a storm to pass if you can dance in the rain instead?'

— Julia Goodfellow-Smith

So, you are progressing nicely towards achieving your dream when WHAM!, you are hit by a storm. At this point, you have a choice: You can allow yourself to be derailed completely; hunker down and wait it out; adapt to it so that you can ride it; or use its power to project you forward. This chapter will help you to consider your options.

My Journey

It was March 2020. I had finally worked up the courage to hand in my notice at work. My confidence had taken a real knock over the last 12 months, so I was giving myself time to lick my wounds, re-build my sense of worth and work out my next plan while walking England's South West Coast Path, a long-held dream. Spring was just around the corner and I was feeling optimistic.

I had a couple of months to train, and then I would hike through the best of the English summer, finishing before the crowds descended in the school holidays.

It was a great plan, but life had other ideas for 2020. A storm with the name coronavirus hit the UK (and the rest of the world) and everything changed.

Not allowed to travel or stay away from home, I walked the Malvern Hills, just a skip and a hop from my house, instead of the coast path. I became lean and tanned, soaking up the sunshine after a long, grey winter. I had a spring in my step. All the aches and pains that I had associated with ageing disappeared almost overnight as I walked ten miles a day.

During this period, I reconnected with nature. People were in lockdown all over the world, but I took heart from knowing that the animals all around us were continuing with their lives as normal, some even flourishing with the reduction in human activity.

Under lockdown conditions, it took me just under three months to complete the same distance and elevation as the South West Coast Path. I loved every minute of it, but I missed the sea. I was aching to hear waves crashing on the shore, taste the salty air, smell the seaweed. I needed more time yet to recover, time alone to reflect, time to dance to the rhythm of the waves.

As lockdown was eased, crowds descended on the South West. Every town, beach, café, pub, bed and campsite was full to the gunnels. To stay safe and to have any chance of finding places to sleep and eat, I would need to wait. Even after the summer rush, I could not be sure of finding places to stay. I would need to carry a tent and be ready to wild camp if I could not find any alternative accommodation. A lightweight walk during the warm, light summer months became a more challenging hike during the cooler, darker autumn months.

By adapting my plans to be able to ride the storm, I actually had a better experience. I walked the distance twice (once in Malvern and once on the South West Coast Path itself), thoroughly enjoying both legs of the journey. I met a far bigger challenge by camping and grew personally much more than I had expected to.

You cannot always see storms coming before they hit. I did not see the coronavirus pandemic coming. Or rather, I did, but I anticipated that it would blow itself out as I had previously seen with outbreaks of SARS and MERS. I certainly did not anticipate country-wide or global lockdowns.

When storms hit that you have not planned for, either metaphorical or real ones, you do not have to just assume that your dreams are over.

There may well be choices available to you. One is to hunker down, stay safe and wait it out.

However, there may well be other options, such as adapting your challenge so that you can ride the storm. I did a combination of both of these. I waited for the crush of people in the South West, caused by the coronavirus pandemic lockdown, to ease before setting off on my walk, and I adapted my walk so that I would be able to complete it despite the conditions created by the pandemic. I also adapted my walk so that I could continue during the worst of Storm Alex.

The night that I camped in the cowpat field was the stormiest, wettest night of my journey so far, although I was snug and dry in my tent. Sticking to the coast path the following day was hard work as the gales buffeted me, my rucksack acting as a sail and amplifying the effect of the wind. I was beginning to think that walking so close to the edge of the cliffs was not a very clever idea when I reached a headland and was stopped dead in my tracks. The wind was so strong that I could not step forward. The only way I could move in the right direction was to sit down and shuffle around the promontory on my bottom. It was definitely time to turn inland and find a safer route to walk.

Later that day, when Storm Alex officially hit the UK, I decided that it would be best to stay in a hotel, rather than take my chances camping. I had adapted my plans again, this time to ride out a literal storm.

Leaving the hotel at St Ives the following morning, I was excited about the day ahead. My destination glowed in a patch of sun at the far end of the bay. I could see that most of the walking would not be dangerous, even in high winds. It was time to take joy in the wildness of the weather and the solitude of walking on my own.

Surfers had flocked down to the first bay I walked past, making the most of the swell caused by the storm. They were battling hard to swim their boards out beyond the powerful breaking waves, but that same force rewarded them with excellent surfing conditions for their precarious ride back into shore.

The next bay is long and wide and designated as a kite-surfing spot. Like the surfers, the kite-surfers were also making the most of the storm. I was mesmerised as I watched them power backwards and forward, travelling in whatever direction they chose, regardless of the direction of the wind. They had found a way to use the power of the storm to travel wherever they chose. What an incredible thing to be able to do!

The surfers and kite-surfers saw the storm as an opportunity, and have learnt to use the power of the storm to their advantage. Many people have used the coronavirus lockdowns to their advantage in different ways too. Some have used the time they have been gifted to learn a new skill, get fit or finally write the book they had been meaning to for years.

The weather conditions did not seem to make any difference to the hunting birds on the trail. On a sunny day, they rode the thermals rising up the cliff faces. On a breezy day, they used the wind to give them lift. And on a stormy day, they seemed to simply adjust their wings more frequently. They soared elegantly and effectively no matter what the conditions. And they maintained their sense of direction and purpose regardless of the bearing of the wind, just like the kite-surfers.

> Having a strong sense of direction and purpose will help you to stay on course, like a hunting bird riding the wind or a kite-surfer riding the waves.

I battled against Storm Alex for a whole week, trying to walk on the coast path, finding it too dangerous and moving inland, then trying again the following day. Camping one night, glad for a building to stay in the next. What was supposed to have been an exciting hike was beginning to feel like a long traipse in the wind and rain.

The coronavirus, having weakened in the UK over the summer months, was becoming more prevalent again, so people were becoming warier of interacting with others and the path became a lonelier place. I was beginning to wonder whether either storm would ever abate.

But, of course, they did. After a week of dark skies and stormy weather, I was astonished — and delighted — to wake to a calm, sunny day. I had fallen asleep to the sound of the wind whipping around the building and rain lashing against the window. I had expected to wake to more of the same. Instead, bright sunshine filtering through the curtains was accompanied by the gentle sound of waves breaking on the beach.

The morning was full of joy. The first time I laughed was when I saw the sun. The second time, it was the foam that had piled up at the shore that tickled me. It wobbled around as if a group of kittens was playing underneath, about to break through. Rounding a headland, I could look back and see the bay I had already walked around. Looking ahead, I could see the coastline sweeping round into the distance until it was just a haze. I laughed again. I was looking forward to walking along that entire length of coastline — and further. What a difference a day makes!

> Sometimes it feels as though storms are never going to end, but they do. Spring follows winter as surely as day follows night, and the sun will shine again after the storm, even if you need to look for it in a slightly different place. If you are lucky, you might even catch a glimpse of a rainbow during the transition.

Your Journey, Step-by-Step

Step 28: Choose your approach to the storm

a) Review your reason why

You might get through the journey to achieving your dream without having to suffer any storms. But if one does hit, review the notes you made when you decided to pursue this dream. What is it that you were particularly excited about when you set off on your journey? What are your reasons why?

b) Identify your options

You might find it useful to use a mind map to identify what options you have for:

- Waiting out the storm. You might have to totally shift your focus to surviving the storm, but if not, how could you productively use this time? Perhaps you could start to plan how to achieve your next dream? Maybe you could sneak achieving a different dream into this space? Or perhaps it would just be a good time to relax and revive.

- Adapting. How can you adapt your route map or dream so that you can complete it, or something very similar, despite the storm?

- Using its power. What opportunities are there to benefit from this situation? How can you use the storm to your advantage?

c) Choose your approach

Consider how attractive each of these options looks to you and choose the one that works best for you at the moment.

Review

You have reached the 'Ride the Storm' waymarker if you have:

- Seen a storm coming or been hit by one unexpectedly.
- Reviewed your reason for pursuing this dream.
- Identified your options for waiting out the storm, adapting or using the power of the storm.
- Chosen your approach to the storm.

Now you have a strategy to adopt if you are hit by a storm. You might need to revisit this waymarker if more than one storm hits while you are pursuing your bucket list dream. If you have done all these things in response to the storm, then you have remained in some degree of control over the situation. Think about how the storm has affected you and how you have reacted. What would you do differently next time?

Make sure that you also celebrate for not allowing yourself to simply be knocked about by the storm. This time, try a fist pump. Raise one hand and bring it in towards your body with a bent elbow, forming a fist and exclaiming 'Yes!' at the same time. Or raise both hands above your head, form fists and pump them up and down.

It does not necessarily take something as powerful as a storm to knock you off course. Even a small gust of wind can change your direction of travel, so as you progress, you will need to check that you are still on the right path and correct your course as needed. The next waymarker will help you do just that.

13

Waymarker 13:

Stay on Track

'My legacy is that I stayed on course...from the beginning to the end, because I believed in something inside of me.'

— Tina Turner, singer

Imagine walking along a straight stretch of path with your eyes closed. If you set off in the right direction, but then do not open your eyes to look at the path again, what would happen? It would not take long for you to veer off in the wrong direction. Every gust of wind or a change in the angle of the path's surface will slightly change your direction of travel. As you walk, you usually make constant small adjustments so that you stay on the path.

It is a similar situation on your journey to achieve your dreams. You need to keep checking that you are heading in the right direction. You might even need to take a detour from time to time. As long as you have the destination in sight and continue to course-correct, you will arrive at the right place.

If you are going to spend a long time travelling to your destination, it makes a lot of sense to enjoy the journey.

This chapter will give you some strategies for making sure that you are on course and that you enjoy the ride.

My Journey

When UK Prime Minister Boris Johnson announced the coronavirus pandemic lockdown, I had mixed feelings. I was relieved because I wanted to stay safe myself and keep others safe too. I was also frustrated because I wanted to achieve my long-held dream of walking the South West Coast Path, and I would not be able to do that during a lockdown. After 25 years of dreaming about walking the path, I had finally decided to do it, and my plans were being thwarted before I had even started training.

I thought back to my 'why'. I needed to escape my sedentary life, and I wanted to serve society. If I walked the same distance and ascent as the South West Coast Path on the Malvern Hills near home, I could still be active and still raise money for the Marine Conservation Society. I could have some fun by wearing a jellyfish costume to draw attention to what I was doing and encourage people to donate. And, it would be a fantastic training regime — when travel restrictions were lifted, I would already be hiking fit. By walking on the Malvern Hills, I would be taking a detour but ultimately still heading towards my dream.

When circumstances change, looking for ways that you can continue heading in the right direction may enable you to make progress, despite the situation. Walking 630 miles on the Malvern Hills was not part of my original plan, but it helped me to achieve some of my 'whys' and to prepare for my actual dream of walking the South West Coast Path.

Every morning, I woke up full of gratitude for living in such a beautiful part of the country with the Malvern Hills on my doorstep. You can stand at the top and feel the Atlantic-fresh air fill your lungs. On other days, it will take your breath away. You can look across the wooded, rolling hills of Herefordshire to the dramatic mountains of the Brecon Beacons in Wales. To the south, on a clear day, you can see the Bristol Channel. Well, Mike and I think that you can. My dad vehemently disagrees! To the east, the River Severn meanders through its broad, flat valley. Usually hidden, the river occasionally reveals itself as a wide ribbon of floodwater, flashing sparkles of light in the morning sun.

From the top of the hills, you can watch the weather marching across the landscape. Bands of clouds, rain and sunshine create a patchwork of light, shade and veiled views.

On very special days, you can walk through the grey murk of a foggy Malvern morning up onto the hills into blazing sunshine, the world below a fluffy blanket of white meringue.

That is how I was lucky enough to spend my lockdown.

Choosing your attitude can change your whole experience of life. Rather than being constantly disappointed about what I could not do, I chose to enjoy what I could do. I looked for things to be grateful for, little things or big things that would fill my heart with joy, like watching the weather sweep across the landscape, seeing the flooded river glinting in the sun or walking up out of the murk and gazing down onto the fluffy white blanket of fog below.

During the summer, while it was still too busy to get to the South West, I walked the Worcestershire Way to practise walking and camping on my own. A few weeks later, just before setting off to the South West, I thought it would be a good idea to walk another local trail, the Three Choirs Way, to keep my level of fitness up and continue to build my confidence with wild camping.

The first day of the walk started positively. The paths along the ridge of the Malvern Hills are well-managed and the weather was mainly fine. But as soon as I left the hills, the path was so badly managed that it was dangerous. I came across stiles that wobbled like see-saws, locked gates, bridges overgrown with spiny brambles and crops planted across the path. I lost count of the number of fences and gates that I had to climb over.

I was wearing the new waterproof boots that I had bought specially for walking the South West Coast Path. I had worn them in over many days of ten-mile walks. However, by mile 15, my feet started to feel uncomfortable. I sat on a patch of grass in the sun and peeled off my socks. My eyes widened in horror. There were two large blisters along the inside of each foot, one on the big toe and the other on the heel. I treated them immediately, so they did not get any worse, but it did not bode well for the longer walk.

That night, the night of my birthday, I camped alone in a camping field. In my excitement that morning, I had forgotten to open my birthday cards. That would have to wait now until I returned. I had planned to meet Mike the following day to look around Gloucester Cathedral together as I walked through, so I would not be on my own for long.

As I was striking camp the next morning, the rain started to fall in lazy sheets. I was not concerned. After all, I had a good waterproof jacket, waterproof trousers and my new waterproof boots. Thinking that I was fully protected from the rain, I set off towards Gloucester, trudging along another series of dangerous and badly maintained footpaths.

By the time I reached the café where I was meeting Mike for breakfast, I was beginning to wonder how waterproof everything really was. It had not rained heavily, but it had been constant for two solid hours.

'You look drenched. You must be freezing. Why don't you sit down and dry your clothes off a bit while I make you a lovely pot of tea?'

As the owner cooked me breakfast, I peeled off my jacket and hung it over the back of a chair to drip-dry. As I had suspected, my shoulders were damp. My jacket was not as waterproof as I had thought. Next, my waterproof over-trousers. Underneath, my legs were dry. Great! And finally, I unlaced my boots and pulled my feet out of them. I felt my socks with my hand. They were damp. So, my new waterproof boots were not waterproof either.

After breakfast, we walked through the cloisters of the cathedral and admired the stained glass windows while I considered my options. Should I stick to my plan and finish walking the Three Choirs Way? Or should I head home and sort out my boots and jacket, so that I could be confident that they would serve me well on the South West Coast Path? There was not enough time for me to do both, so I had to make a decision.

The purpose of walking the Three Choirs Way had been to further prepare for the South West Coast Path. It was the means to an end, not the end in itself. It was time to change my plans, head home, and get it all sorted out before I left.

The planning and adjustments to plans did not end when I started walking the South West Coast Path a few days later. Every night, I pored over the maps, checked the weather forecast, and thought about where I would be able to find food and campsites over the next few days. Every day, I tweaked my plan as conditions changed, so that I would continue heading in the right direction.

Keeping an eye on your overall aim helps you to make decisions that keep you on track.

In terms of fundraising, a period of pandemic is not a great time to be asking people for money. Businesses had to close for extended periods, and a lot of people were not sure how long they would have a job for. People were not carrying cash because nowhere was open to spend it, and they were avoiding close contact with others. All of this combined to make me realise that my £10,000 fundraising goal was not likely to be achieved.

I checked in with myself. Would I feel as though I had cheated if I reduced my target? The extreme change in circumstances meant that I did not. So, I privately adjusted my expectations and decided that I would consider the walk a success if I had raised £5,000. Which I did – just!

If conditions change significantly, revisiting some elements of your ambitions might be a good idea. Remember, this is your bucket list dream and you can redefine it at any time. As long as you feel that it is a reasonable adjustment, then it is.

'Did you know that it's a good idea to look backwards sometimes to see how far you have come? People who do that are far more likely to finish a hike than those who just look ahead and think about how much more they need to do.'

Early on in my walk, my friend Hazel, who gave me this gem of advice, walked with me for a few days. I thought that it could not do any harm, so tried it out. It certainly worked for me. On the days when I was tired and could see how hard the next few miles' walking would be, I would turn round and look at the coastline behind me disappearing into the distance. I found it reassuring. I had walked that long and winding trail, so I must be able to walk what was ahead.

Waymarkers on the path also gave me a sense of progression. Most of them just mark the route of the path or the distance to the next town, but occasionally, they have the miles to the path's start and finish points. These are the ones that I looked forward to seeing.

I almost walked past the first one without noticing. Poole 168 miles, Minehead 462 miles. I gave myself a pat on the back. I had already walked for 168 miles! And I was delighted to know that I had so many more to go. As I left Clovelly, it was Poole 531 miles, Minehead 99 miles. I had walked over 500 miles. Little old me! Who would have thought it? And I had less than 100 miles to go. I was on the home straight.

Waymarkers on the path are like the stages you have set up for achieving your dream.

Once each stage is complete, looking back to see what you have achieved and allowing yourself a moment for celebration will give you a boost to head forward.

Looking forward and taking a moment to consider how lucky you are to be able to pursue your bucket list will add to that boost.

Even if it is just a little positive thought, your brain likes to receive a reward and subconsciously drives you to do more of the same so that you get more of that great feeling. So, praising or rewarding yourself along the way and being grateful for the opportunities you have can give you a real incentive to carry on.

Your Journey, Step-by-Step

Step 29: List your rewards

List 10 rewards that you can give yourself as you progress towards your goal, plus one big one for achieving your goal. They can be small rewards or big rewards. The important thing is that they must feel like rewards to you.

Step 30: Check you are still heading in the right direction

a) Review each stage

As you come to start each of your stages, take a few moments to reflect. Does that stage still take you in the right direction? Can the step-by-step plan be tweaked for it to become more effective or more fun?

b) Review steps and congratulate yourself

As you complete each step, take a few more moments to reflect. Congratulate yourself for taking action. This could just be a thought, or even better, give yourself a real pat on the back. It is guaranteed to make you smile! Once you have congratulated yourself, think about whether it was a worthwhile step. Did it take you in the right direction, or just take up your time? This is all a process of learning and honing our planning and execution skills.

c) Look back as you complete each stage

When you have completed each stage of your journey, take a moment to look back over the process. What have you learnt about yourself? Has that part of the journey been effective in moving you towards achieving your dream? What can you learn and apply to the rest of your route map?

Once you have done this, remember to reward yourself again. Pick a reward from the list you created in the last step, and enjoy your moment of celebration before moving on to the next step.

d) Look forward to what is to come

Rather than just thinking about what still needs to be done, consider briefly how lucky you are to be in a position to be able to pursue your dream.

e) Update your route map

Once you have completed your reflections, update your route map, stages and step-by-step plans if you need to.

f) Review your dream

When you have completed a stage, this is also a good time to review the details of your dream that you created in Waymarker 1. Does anything there need tweaking?

Review

You have reached the 'Stay on Track' waymarker if you have:

- Identified rewards for yourself that will help you to stay motivated.
- Reviewed each of your stages when you started it and when you completed it.

- Rewarded yourself for each step you have taken and stage you have completed.

If you have completed all of these steps, congratulations! You have stayed on course and achieved your bucket list dream and reached the 'Achieve your Dream' milestone – congratulations!

Achieving your dream is not the end of your journey, though. There is one more milestone to reach yet. If you just tick your dream off your bucket list and move on, you will have missed an important part of the process and your triumph may be short-lived.

The final waymarker and milestone provides you with a tool to consolidate your memories, what you have learnt and who you have become on the journey.

Milestone Four:

Reflect

Waymarker 14:

Celebrate and Reflect

'It's not about the goal. It's about growing to become the person that can accomplish the goal.'

—— Tony Robbins, #1 New York Times bestselling author, philanthropist and #1 life and business strategist

Congratulations! You are living your bucket list and have achieved one of your dreams. Before your attention is diverted to other things, take some time to celebrate and reflect on your experience.

My Journey

When I passed the waymarker at Clovelly that told me I had less than 100 miles to go, I could envisage the end of my journey. On my final day's hike, the fog cleared just enough for me to see the sculpture marking the end of the path while I was still on top of the cliffs. My legs were heavy and my breath was laboured as I walked down the hill towards it.

I recognised the magnificence of the moment, but could not help myself thinking, 'Is this it?' as I posed for photos. I had waited for this moment for 25 years; I had finally achieved my dream. I was proud of what I had achieved – after all, it was a far bigger challenge than I had set out to do – yet the elation was tinged with a great big dollop of disappointment.

I had initially planned to throw a party for friends, family and other supporters at that final waymarker, but alas, parties were totally out of the question during the pandemic. Instead, three of us celebrated with a fish and chip lunch in a local pub.

Over the next few weeks, I reflected on my experience. I realised that it was the journey itself and the person I became on the way that were the most important things to me. That final moment of completion was just one of many victories to be celebrated.

I had learnt practical things about camping and backpacking that I could either apply or avoid doing in the future. More than that, though, I had learnt a lot that I could apply to my life more broadly.

One evening a couple of weeks into my journey, I stayed at a beautiful campsite on a hill above the coast. The tents, caravans and campervans were all well-spaced, and Johnny, the campsite warden, showed me to a pitch on lovely soft grass, close to the pond.

'Do you have any dinner with you?' I assured him that I did.

'If you'd like some company tonight, my door is always open.'

I pitched my tent, occasionally looking up to watch the swans gliding serenely across the water. As I waited for my dinner to cook, the sun slunk below the horizon, shimmering its golden light across the bucolic scene.

By 8 p.m., it was totally dark. I was camping on my own, and the temperature was dropping rapidly. I thought about Johnny's offer of company, but I was not sure whether to accept. Maybe he was not serious, and I would be foisting myself on him. Or, even worse, maybe he was serious and had an ulterior motive. Maybe he was a raging axe murderer who targeted lone female campers. Should I take the risk?

Eventually, the temptation of company and somewhere warm, dry and comfortable to spend the evening won out over the fear of embarrassment or worse. I took the plunge, and I am glad I did. Johnny was a delight.

I sat near the open door of his living quarters, drank tea and listened to his stories of how he found his place in the universe. He talked about being miserable trying to keep up with the Jones', his road to enlightenment in India, how he discovered that everything is love, and the respect that he has for the conspiracy theorist, David Icke. It was a slightly surreal evening, but so much better than whiling away the hours in my tent, sitting alone in the dark.

As an introvert, I find talking to strangers very stressful, although I recognise the benefit of doing so. I had promised myself that I would talk to as many people as possible during my journey, and this strategy turned out well. One way or another, by simply striking up conversation with people, I received multiple gifts from strangers, including Johnny, that made the journey far more enjoyable.

One sunny morning, I was waiting in a queue when I noticed that the man next to me was wearing an army gas mask. At this point, everyone was wearing a face mask as a protection against coronavirus, but generally, these were just made from cloth. His covered his whole face and was made from black rubber, with clear lenses in front of his eyes and a respirator protruding to one side. Overall, the effect was rather sinister. Two voices competed in my head.

'You said you were going to speak to everyone you met. Say hello to him.'

And the other, slightly panicky, 'There's no way you should speak to that man. Wearing a gas mask like that, he is probably even more dangerous than an axe-wielding murderer!'

A few deep breaths later, I worked up the courage to strike up a conversation with him.

'My parents used to display army kit from the 1980s at shows, so they have whole nuclear, chemical and biological protective suits at home. When we were told to wear face masks, I thought that this would be more effective than a cloth one.'

He was probably right, and apart from his rather unusual attire, he seemed to be perfectly normal. Unlike the man who sidled over while we were talking.

He was also intrigued by the gas mask, but for different reasons. It reminded him of an episode of Doctor Who when a child had a gas mask fused to his face to help him to heal. After that, all his descendents were born with black masks over their faces.

After regaling us with the plots and sub-plots of Doctor Who, he showed me a photo on his mobile phone and asked me whether I recognised it. It looked like a communications tower to me, not something that I have a special interest in, and I would certainly not be able to distinguish one from another. When he told me that it was the transmitter for a chemical plant warning siren in the United States, I was even more baffled about why he might expect me to recognise it.

As he played me siren after siren, explaining the difference between them, I was beginning to look for a way out of the conversation. And then, I heard a siren that I recognised. I was instantly transported back to my childhood home. As I was growing up, I had heard this siren being tested every week, a two-tone noise for a couple of minutes followed by a monotone all-clear.

It was used to signal an escape from a local high-security prison, and occasionally it was sounded for real. Whenever I heard it when it was not a test, my heart sank. Until the prisoner was back behind bars, we would not be able to play in the woods or walk to our friends' houses without an adult. I always hoped that the prisoner would be found quickly, not so that we would be safe again, but so that we could have our usual freedoms reinstated.

What a blast from the past, and an unexpected moment to have on a warm September morning, about to embark on another day's walking of the South West Coast Path. I would never have expected that I would be sandwiched between one man wearing a gas mask, and another playing prison escape sirens to me on his phone!

I still find it hard to talk to people, but I know that overcoming my reluctance is sometimes the right thing to do and can also lead to some wonderful moments like these.

Having done very little on my own in the past, I also learnt about how, as an introvert, time on my own helps me to recharge.

Spending so much time on my own, I have become more confident in my decision-making and problem-solving abilities. This journey also helped me to see that I am more resilient and more determined than I knew.

And I have a plethora of amazing memories from the year that I will be able to draw on for the rest of my life. If I ever need to cheer myself up, I will be able to imagine what it was like sitting on the beach with my rucksack, listening to the sea sucking between the pebbles, gently knocking them together. If I ever need to feel safe, I will be able to imagine the feeling of security as I zip up the door to my tent and climb into my sleeping bag, with everything I need to hand. If I ever need a release from fear or anger, I will be able to take myself back to that cairn on the top of Great Hangman, calling blessings out into the wind. And if I ever doubt my courage, I will be able to remember my sheer bloody-minded determination to finish the path, even though I was really quite ill.

It is only in reflection that I have realised how much I have learnt – and how much I have changed.

Achieving your dreams is as much about the journey as the destination. The triumphant feeling of achieving your goal might not last for long, but the skills you have gained, the things you have learnt about yourself and others, and who you have become on the journey will stay with you forever.

Taking time to reflect at the end of your journey will help you to realise all these additional elements of your achievement.

In writing about my experiences and creating presentations about my journey, I have done a lot to consolidate many special memories. I have had to sort through my photos and pick out those that best represent my journeys – both physical and emotional. I have had to relive so many of my experiences that this trip will remain clear in my mind for the rest of my life.

Reviewing your journey, each of the stages that you completed and who you had to become to get there will help you to remember significant moments and feelings. If you take the time to do this, you will gain so much more from the whole experience.

Your Journey, Step-by-Step

Step 31: Reflect on your journey

Once you have achieved your dream, take some time to reflect. A mind map might come in useful again here.

a) Consider what has changed

What skills have you developed? What have you learnt about yourself? What have you learnt about others? How have you changed? How have you changed the lives of others?

b) Apply what you have learnt

Now think about how you can apply each of these things to your everyday life. Make a note of any changes that you would like to make to further strengthen yourself or integrate these things into your daily routine.

Step 32: Celebrate!

a) Reward yourself

Go back to your list of rewards and pick your favourite to celebrate your success. Or maybe you could throw a celebratory party. Do whatever works for you to praise your achievement.

b) Create a congratulatory certificate

Use wording along the lines of: "I, NAME, have started to live my bucket list, by achieving my dream to XX. In the process of achieving my dream, I have grown my confidence and learnt XX."

Print it out and hang it on the wall in place of the certificate you created in step 22.

Download a free template for this certificate from: www.juliags.com/liveyourbucketlist

c) Strengthen your memories

Create a photo book from your experience, or a photo montage, painting or patchwork panel of your achievement. Or write a book about your experience. Books can just be for your own enjoyment, they do not have to be made available to the public. Do whatever works for you to settle your memories.

Step 33: Tell us all about it

Post a photo of your certificate/photo montage/end of challenge party to www.facebook.com/groups/liveyourbucketlist-now/. Inspire other people with what you have achieved, what you have learnt – and what you are going to do next!

Step 34: Start planning your next bucket list adventure

It is official. You are now living your bucket list. This means that, once you have finished reflecting and celebrating, it is time to start planning your next bucket list adventure.

a) Review your list

- Are there some more challenging things that you would like to add now that you have gained confidence and skills?

- Are there ways that you would like to use your new-found skills and confidence to support your community or the wider world?
- Are there things that you would like to take off the list?
- Has this time of reflection refocused your priorities? Your bucket list is not about bragging rights, but about living an extraordinary life of passion in line with your values.

b) Repeat the process

Head back to Waymarker 1 and start your next bucket list journey.

Conclusion

You have reached the 'Celebrate and Reflect' waymarker and the 'Implementation' milestone, which also marks the end of this particular journey, when you have:

- Reflected on your experience and what it has meant to you and others.
- Integrated changes into your everyday life to maximise the ongoing benefit from your experience.
- Celebrated your success.
- Strengthened your memories.
- Told our Facebook community all about it.

Congratulations – what an achievement!
What are you going to do next?

As you work through this book again for your next bucket list dream, please be prepared for things to be different. You are probably not quite the same person you were when you started this journey. You might find that you no longer have the same limiting beliefs, or you might have unearthed some others that you want to crush. You might find that different mantras will be needed to get you through a different sort of challenge.

This time around, it will also be different because you already know that you can achieve your dreams if you apply this process to them.

I recommend that you start again from the beginning and use the whole process. You might even look at your old bucket list and add and subtract a few items, to keep things fresh.

Living my bucket list has been an incredible ride. There have been all sorts of twists and turns, thrills and moments of terror. All of these have made my life richer and strengthened my inner self. They have helped me to contribute more and make the world a better place.

I hope that your journey has been equally as thrilling and equally as rewarding.

Now, what is next?

An Invitation

Thank you for reading my book! I really appreciate receiving feedback so that I can make the next version of this book and my future books better. I love hearing what you have to say — please leave me an honest review on Amazon letting me know what you thought of the book.

Join us at www.facebook.com/groups/liveyourbucketlist-now/ for ongoing encouragement and support for living your bucket list.

For free templates to accompany *Live Your Bucket List*, go to: www.juliags.com/liveyourbucketlist

If you have found my stories entertaining and would like to hear more, please stay in touch:

www.juliags.com

🇫 @juliagsadventure

📷 @juliagsadventure

▶ Julia Goodfellow-Smith

If you are looking for an entertaining and inspiring speaker for a meeting, event or broadcast, please give me a shout. julia@ juliags.com

I have published this book with the support of Self-Publishing School. If writing a book is on your bucket list, they can help you to become a best-selling author in as little as three months. Go to https://self-publishingschool.com/friend/ for a free resource to get you started and to unlock a special discount.

Thank you so much!

Acknowledgements

I would like to start by thanking my husband Mike. Without his support and encouragement, I might never have walked the South West Coast Path, and I would not have written this book.

To all the people who walked with me, thank you so much for your time and encouragement.

Hazel — here's to dinner with strangers who become friends.

Phil, Chris and Nige — what a wonderful day and a fantastic finish!

Maggie and Ian — you really gave me a boost the day we met, just when I needed it. Thank you.

Alison — doggie ice cream, anyone?

Tim — I hope the weather is kinder to you next time.

Jim, Arthur (Artie) and other long-distance walkers — may a gentle breeze always be on your back and the sun on your face.

To everyone who gave me a meal and/or somewhere comfortable to sleep. You have no idea how much that meant to me.

Andy at the Veterans' Hub — keep up the good work.

Carl and Richard — what a hoot!

Jo — let's not leave it so long next time.

Jane and Dave — please give Hercules a hug from me.

Jacqui, Doug and Ella — loved the custard!

Carol at Pennant Farm near Port Isaac — delicious lasagne and gorgeous slippers!

Margot — your timing was perfect.

Rudi Lancaster and all the staff and other visitors at Woolacombe Bay Holiday Park — for keeping me safe and making kindness shine brighter than anger.

For the final day of my walk on the Malverns, the Marine Conservation Society lent me the best costumes ever. Thank you Ali for bending the rules ever-so-slightly, and to Hazel, Paul and Mike for willingly dressing up as a starfish, cod and turtle and making me laugh so much that my cheeks ached.

And to everyone else who supported me along the path, who are too numerous to list, including those who donated to the Marine Conservation Society. Thank you for your generosity – of spirit and purse.

Self-publishing is an adventure on its own. Thank you to the Self-Publishing School and my coach Brett Hilker in particular, for helping me to navigate my way through the process. Fern, you have been an incredible accountability buddy, always encouraging me and offering gems of advice and help.

Jon Doolan — thank you for offering me invaluable advice as my editor, as well as knocking my English into shape. Death to extraneous commas! Thank you too to Alejandro Martin for a fabulous cover and layout.

And last, but not least, thank you to everyone on my launch team for buying a copy of *Live Your Bucket List* as soon as it was published and leaving me reviews. You know who you are. You have made a world of difference to me and every other reader by sharing your thoughts.

About the Author

Julia Goodfellow-Smith is an ordinary person who is doing something extraordinary — living her bucket list. She would like to help others do the same, which is why she has written this book.

She has held a variety of management and consultancy roles in a range of sectors including conservation volunteering, banking and construction. She is currently focusing her attention on adventure, writing and presenting.

Julia lives close to the Malvern Hills with her husband Mike. She spends a lot of time either wandering on the hills or working in their small woodland nearby. She is a member of the Women's Institute and Toastmasters International, a Fellow of the Royal Society of Arts and a Senator of Junior Chamber International (JCI).